MARRIAGE RECORD
OF
WASHINGTON COUNTY, TENNESSEE

1787 - 1840

Compiled by
Norma Rutledge Grammer
and
Marion Day Mullins

CLEARFIELD

Originally published
[Fort Worth, 1949]

Reprinted with permission by
Genealogical Publishing Company
Baltimore, Maryland
1973

Reprinted for
Clearfield Company by
Genealogical Publishing Company
Baltimore, Maryland
2008

Library of Congress Catalogue Card Number 73-8035
ISBN 978-0-8063-0564-6

Made in the United States of America

MARRIAGE RECORD

Washington County, Tennessee

Date	Male	Female	Bondman
Sept. 19, 1787	Archer Evans—Charlotte Cooper.		Wm. Cobb
Dec. 26, 1787	Champ Guin—Dorcas Williams.		Arthur Burke
Dec. 27, 1787	George Gabbert—Catherine Smith.		Isaac Grindstaff
Jan. 12, 1788	Thomas Love—Martha Dillard.		Thos. Dillard
Jan. 17, 1788	John Rodgers—Elizabeth Asher.		David Asher
Jan. 20, 1788	Joel Cooper—Elizabeth Job.		Job Cowper
Jan. 25, 1788	Samuel Apperson—Milly Holland.		James Nowland
Feb. 1, 1788	Samuel Underwood—Mary Shearer.		Robert Young
Feb. 7, 1788	John Smith—Jemima Grimes.		Alexander Moffet
Feb. 25, 1788	Arthur Burke—Mary Anderson.		John Anderson
Mar. 25, 1788	Charles McCrea—Betsy Dickens.		William Noding
Mar. 27, 1788	Daniel Allon—Allathy Hale.		Isaac Denton
May 7, 1788	John Beaty—Ann Wood.		Isaac Depew
Aug. 6, 1788	Caleb Oddie—Peggy Borring.		William Borring
Aug. 11, 1788	John Shaw—Mary Irwin.		John Gaut
Aug. 19, 1788	Charles Bickley—Mary Hatler.		Joseph Martin
Sept. 3, 1788	Thompkin Oddie—Abigail Combs.		Jacob Tipton
Sept. 10, 1788	Daniel Blevins—Agnes Postlethwait.		John Hays
Oct. 8, 1788	Andrew Hannah—Jane Davis.		Ambrose Yancey
Dec. 1, 1788	Caleb Odell—Jane McDaniel.		Abraham Burgham
Dec. 3, 1788	Brooks Smith—Rebecca Daniels.		John Daniels
Feb. 5, 1789	Notty Williams—Ruth Collins.		William Hamilton
Feb. 16, 1789	Robert Campble—Anne Campble.		John Campbell
Feb. 18, 1789	John Tate—Elizabeth Parkeson.		Peter Parkeson
Feb. 23, 1789	James Campbell—Rebekah Linville.		Jeremiah Campbell
May 6, 1789	Benjamin Brown—Sarah Sevier.		John G. Brown
July 18, 1789	James Nowlan—Mary Holland.		George Nolen, bro.
Sept. 12, 1789	Jeremiah Campbell—Sarah Marr.		William Davis
Sept. 22, 1789	John Taylor—Rachel Hannah.		John Edwards
Oct. 28, 178.	Hugh Rodgers—Nancy Thornton.		Edmund Williams
Nov. 5, 1789	John Hetherly—Nancy Wilson.		George Terril
Nov. 18, 1789	James Graves—Sarah Hetherly.		Sam Tate
Nov. 21, 1789	James Lacy—Nancy Edden.		John Daniels
Dec. 14, 1789	John McInturff, Jr.—Judith Carder.		John McInturff, Sr.
Dec. 22, 1789	John Knight—Rebecca Rhodes.		Elisha Bellemey
Jan. , 179.	William Gilles—Carson.		James Campbell
Jan. 5, 1790	Adam Simerly—Hannah Nowaland.		Ezekial Able

Date	Male	Female	Bondman
Jan. 6, 1790	John Hatcher—Eve Moris		Juniston Hatcher
April 21, 1790	Thomas Dunkin—Mary Lynch		
May 10, 1790	Samuel Carson—Rebekah Brandon		Nat'l. Davis
Sept. 1, 1790	John Lucas—Sussanah Hale		John Tipton
Sept. 13, 1790	Cheney Boring—Elizabeth White Cotton		
			John Tipton
Oct. 4, 1790	Harris Wylie—Arty Taylor		Robert Wyley
Nov. 3, 1790	John Bitner—Elizabeth Hatter		Adam Painter
Nov. 11, 1790	Phillip Waggoner—Catherine Follon		Evan Dobkin
Nov. 11, 1790	Andrew Carson—Elizabeth Hannah		Moris Carson
Jan. 18, 1791	William Crawford—Rebeckah Smith		Anderson Smith
Jan. 23, 1791	Jonathan Carreathers—Sarah Young		Robert Young
Jan. 26, 1791	George Little—Marey Job		Isaac Tipton
Feb. 8, 1791	David Conklin—Marey Graham		William Green
Feb. 13, 1791	Ethelred Cobb—Susanah McColm		Archer Evans
Feb. 15, 1791	John Willson—Sarah Winberg		W. C. Flannary
Feb. 19, 1791	William Shanks—Elizabeth Roberson		
			John Campbell
Mar. 16, 1791	Baultis Hamer—Sarah Carney		John Carney
Mar. 16, 1791	James Law—Rosanah Talford		Samuel Shaw
Mar. 26, 1791	William Dewoody—Hanah Alexander		John Alexander
April 9, 1791	John Meginnis—Ann Tucker		George Evans
July 23, 1791	Thomas Tipton—Rebekah Lacy		Samuel Tipton
July 30, 1791	James Smith—Ehster McDonald		
			Thomas B. Rutherford
Aug. 9, 1791	William Duggard—Nancy Millar		Thomas Millar
Sept. 14, 1791	John William Wheat—Mary Williams		George House
Jan. 13, 1792	William Crawford—Rebecca Smith		Daniel Dunn
Jan. 16, 1792	Elijah Crouch—Mary Ellis		William Crabtree
Mar. 12, 1792	Charl Stuart—Mary Blair		M. Harrison
May 27, 1792	David McCord—Susana Carson		
May 3, 1792	John Leach—Sarah Solomon		Lewis Jordan
June 25, 1792	David Stuart—Ann Allison		Nat Cowan
July 14, 1792	Robert Fryer—Chaestain Hunter		Samuel Bayles
Aug. 23, 1792	Jesse Keel—Mary North		James Keele
Aug. 30, 1792	Nathan Wilkinson—Rebeckah Wear		John Embree
Sept. 5, 1792	Stephen Redman—Susanna Stewart		Wm. Forrester
Sept. 23, 1792	Samuel Kenady—Lett Herrold		Richard Jones
Oct. 12, 1792	James Twedy— Blakely		David Bleakley
Oct. 16, 1792	John Slyger—Mary Harmon		
Nov. 15, 1792	Sebastine Hedler—Elizabeth Kerselas		John Bitner
Jan. 2, 1793	James Price—Esther Noland		John Price
Jan. 12, 1793	John Tipton—Sarah Murey		Abraham Borin

Date	Male	Female	Bondman
Feb. 5, 1793	Thomas House—Ann Davison		George House
Feb. 13, 1793	John Gott—Mary Evans		John Hammer
Feb. 23, 1793	Samuel Lain—Elisateh Hunt		John Eton
Mar. 5, 1793	Andrew Gammil—Gannat Carson		Moses Carson
Mar. 19, 1793	Josiah Ballinger—Elizabeth Smith		Isaac Embree
Mar. 19, 1793	Samuel Lamon—Mary Allon		James Charter
Mar. 20, 1793	James Rodgers—Rhoda Alexander		Samuel Davis
Mar. 26, 1793	Arnold Green—Rebecca Messer		Joshua Green
April 23, 1793	Garrett Reasoner—Margarett Rennor		Joseph Tipton
April 29, 1793	Michal Ingle—Mary Slyger		William Ingle
May 23, 1793	George Dearmond—Nancy Webb		Cottrel Beily
May 27, 1793	Littleberry Samms—Elizabeth Burns		John Samms
May 29, 1793	Isaac Hammer—Elizabeth Bogart		Samuel Bogart
June 14, 1793	Alexander Hall—Susanah McColam		James Hall
July 8, 1793	William Keele—Levinah Bewley		John Keele
July 13, 1793	Robert Rogers—Hanna Tipton		John Tipton
Aug. 27, 1793	Cornelas Bogart—Elisabeth Moffet		John McIntury
Sept. 9, 1793	John McConal—Agnes Trotter		Samuel Cowan
Sept. 9, 1793	Joseph Trotter—Jane Carmichael		Nathinel Cowan
Sept. 26, 1793	William McGee—Leoma Booyle		Reuben Booyle
Oct. 5, 1793	Absolem Boren—Hannah Litle		Abraham Cox
Nov. 6, 1793	John Bradley—Nancy Tate		Samuel Tate
Nov. 13, 1793	James Nasbit—Sarah Logan		
Nov. 18, 1793	John McCoy—Hannah Lusk		N. Taylor
Nov. 26, 1793	John Blair—Hannah Carreathers		Robert Maclen
Nov. 26, 1793	John Watson—Christianna Headerick		Jonathan Watson
Dec. 2, 1793	Robert Henry—Mary Campbell		James Campbell
Dec. 21, 1793	James Roddey—Elizabeth Houston		David Tate
Dec. 24, 1793	David Robertson—Sarah Currey		Joseph McCorkle
Dec. 25, 1793	Edward West—Elizabeth Humphreys		George Humphreys
Dec. 30, 1793	Joseph McCorkle—Jean Harrison		David Robinson
Jan. 22, 1794	William Burk—Elizabeth Thompson		David Conley
Feb. 8, 1794	James Ritchey—Sarah Carson		David Carson
Feb. 27, 1794	James Hunter—Jane McCord		James McCord
Mar. 3, 1794	Babtist McNabb— Gray		Andrew Taylor
April 22, 1794	Samuel Cowan—Jean Montgomery		John Waddill Jr.
April 26, 1794	David Carson—Marey Burke		John Waddill, Jr.
April 26, 1794	William Lashbrooks—Dorratha Cressealeas		Sebastian Hitler
June 4, 1794	James Penny—Mary McFarland		Andrew Beard
July 7, 1794	Raleigh Duncan—Mary Keer		Thomas Davis

Date	Male	Female	Bondman
Aug. 6, 1794	John Payne—Rachel Parker		Reuben Payne
Aug. 26, 1794	James Ranken—Mary Breser		J. Rees
Aug. 27, 1794	Joseph Willson—Sarah Cutbert		Joseph Ford
Sept. 13, 1794	John Gilles—Ann Ginkens		George Ginkins
Sept. 19, 1794	Jacob Robertson—Elizabeth Wheelock		John Wheelock
Sept. 23, 1794	Elihu Burt—Mary Garret		
Sept. 30, 1794	Alaxander Frazer—Charrity Bass		Jno. Sumerlin
Oct. 6, 1794	John Parker—Margarett Cashedy		Dareling Jones
Dec. 17, 1794	John Blair—Margaret Blair		A. Samuel Blair
Dec. 26, 1794	William Chapman—Elizabeth Henderson		Thomas Pearson
Dec. 31, 1794	David Deaderick—Margaretta Anderson		James Stuart
Jan. 27, 1795	Nathaniel Davis—Elizabeth Celso		
Feb. 27, 1795	Jonathan Tipton—		George House
Feb. 28, 1795	John Rolston—Mary Shanks		
May 21, 1795	William Ray—Franky Russell		Joseph Ford
June 3, 1795	Garland Willson—Mary Cook		
July 20, 1795	Robert Carson—Jane Ritchey		John Carson
Aug. 3, 1795	George Sheffield—Mary Little		George House
Aug. 9, 1795	Anthony Patten—Elizabeth Matthews		John Adams
Aug. 25, 1795	James Eagin—Hannah Whitson		Charles Whitson
Oct. 15, 1795	William Brown—Catherine Sweet		David Brown
Dec. 28, 179..	Edward Weston—Elizabeth Humphres		Moses Humphreys
Jan. 29, 1796	David Richey—Elizabeth McCord		James McCord
Feb. 13, 1796	Benjamin McNut—Amy Alexander		Alexander Purden
April 21, 1796	Alexander Forguson—Mary McNutt		
May 25, 1796	David Pugh—Rachel Bogard		William Pugh
Sept. 19, 1796	Henry McCray—Marey More		Charles McCray
Sept. 20, 1796	James Seehorn—Agness McWhorter		Samuel Davis
Sept. 21, 1796	Chana Boren—Mary Pearcefield		James Moore
Sept. 21, 1796	John Macanelly—Jemima Jackson		William Jackson
Dec. 1, 1796	John Mitchell—Mary Ann Barnes		William Mitchell
Dec. 6, 1796	John McCord—Mary Carson		John McCord
Dec. 30, 1796	Phillip Brown—Catherine Sliger		Solomon Brown
Mar. 30, 1797	Solomon Brown—Mary Bayless		Abraham Brown
June 19, 1797	Joshua Edwards—Mary Bide		William King
July 14, 1797	Jeremiah Brown—Catherine Gyer		George Evans
Sept. 19, 1797	George Hail, Jr.—Ellenor Chamberlain		J. Britten
Sept. 27, 1797	William Insor—Martha Lasly		Peter Shipley

4

Date	Male	Female	Bondman
Oct. 10, 1797	William Bayles—Catherine Hare		
Nov. 6, 1797	John Ewing—Martha Campbell		Hugh Campbell
Dec. 2, 1797	James Willcox—Sarah Doan		Nicholas Spring
Dec. 4, 1797	Adam Slieger—Catherine Brown		Philip Brown
Dec. 10, 1797	William Hale—Mary Fernsworth		James Hale
Dec. 16, 1797	Jacob Gates—Elizabeth Genkins		
Jan. 20, 1798	Joseph Boyd—Phebe Little		Edward Makin
Feb. 28, 1798	James Winders—Jean Forbush		David Robison
June 22, 1798	Adam Broyles—Rosannah Broyles		Nathan Gan
Aug. 19, 1798	John Morrison—Sarah Embry		Nathaniel Spring
Sept. 2, 1798	Richard Kayhill—Elizabeth Anderson		James Roberts
Sept. 5, 1798	Martin Cleek—Merrianna Borders		Malchi Cleek
Dec. 1, 1798	James Reed—Sally Hicky		Edward Mackin
Dec. 22, 1798	John Murr—Mary Brown		John Brown
Feb. 16, 1799	Henry Osmas—Linda Price		Joshua Boran
Feb. 16, 1799	Daniel Robison—Polly Ritchie		James Blair
Mar. 18, 1799	Joshua Tipton—Rechal Hagan		James Denton
April 11, 1799	Thomas Mitchell—Fanny Tucker		Richard Blair
April 20, 1799	Abraham Bogart—Elisabeth Duncan		
			Marshall Duncan
May 7,	John Stanton—Margaret Piveley		Robert Blair
May 8, 1799	John Cash—Hannah Dosser		Martin Sidner
Sept. 25, 1799	Lewis White—Ruth Carson		David Carson
Brt. 1805 & 1815	—John Cole—Catherine Layman		Emanuel Layman
Jan. 22, 1800	James Hill—Hannah Carter		Daniel Gann
April 29, 1800	William Sullins—Mary Reed		John Irwin
July 27, 1801	David Fawbush—Sally Grills		Hugh Fawbush
Aug. 22, 1801	Walter Chase—Elizabeth Murray		Jeremiah Chase
Aug. 31, 1801	Cornelius Morgan—Jenny Hosier		Charles Morgan
Sept. 2, 1801	Elijah Hathway—Elisabeth Crouch		John Lyon
Sept. 5, 1801	Joseph Brown—Betsy Alexander		John Alexander
Sept. 15, 1801	Isaiah Riggs—Ruth Murry		William Odeneal
Sept. 15, 1801	Thomas Hagan—Nancy Birdwell		Arthur Hagan
Jan. 5, 1802	John Blakley—Priscilla Oneneal		Othniel Sands
Mar. 31, 1802	Joseph Kyser—Jane Boothe		Eli Edwards
Sept. ...., 1802	James Pewit—Catharine Andes		John Smith
April 19, 1803	Joseph Byler—Rebeccah Dillard		John Dillard
July 27, 1803	Joseph Tilson—Nancy Tompkins		Gabriel McInturff
July 20, 1803	John Baze—Agnes Harbison		Michael Harrison
Aug. 23, 1803	Frederick Dewalt—Margarett Range		
			Nicholas Keefhaver
Aug. 24, 1803	Christian Winkler—Hannah Smilser		
			Benjemin Overstek

Date	Male	Female	Bondman
Aug. 26, 1803	Jesse Payne, Jr.—Mary Newman		
Dec. 17, 1803	Jonathen Waddill—Hannah Greenway		John Huston
Mar. 30, 1804	John McEwen—Eliza Stephenson		David Patten
Mar. 21, 1805	Barney Burns—Mary Embree		
June 10, 1805	Thomas W. Smith—Rebeckah Mitchell		
			William Mitchell
July 16, 1805	Thomas Mitchell—Polly Million		
July 25, 1805	Reuben Burk—Polly Lyons		
Sept. 16, 1805	James Mitchell—Sally Starnes		
Oct. 3, 1805	Jacob Brown—Nancy Thompson		
Oct. 10, 1805	Edward Million—Sally Mitchell		
Nov. 21, 1805	Jacob Fellers—Hannah Brown		
Dec. 5, 1805	Thomas Charlton—Jenny Glass		
Jan. 25, 1806	Peter Smitzer—Sally Clabaugh		
Mar. 3, 1806	Jesse Mullins—Betsy Tadlock		
Mar. 9, 1806	Alexander Erwin—Sally Bacon		
Mar. 26, 1806	Benjamin Price—Polly Denton		
June 21, 1806	William Bleakley—Margaret Taylor		
Aug. 12, 1806	James Moore—Mary Clarke		Othneal Sands
Aug. 16, 1806	William Mares—Elizabeth Stephens		
			Brice M. Garner
Aug. 23, 1806	William McCall—Thency Shields		
Sept. 13, 1806	Butler Hail—Betsy Messer		Leroy Hail
Nov. 18, 1806	David Besset—Anny Hickman		Monty Stuart
Nov. 20, 1806	John Rankin—Jane Weir		Benjamin Blackburn
Dec. 4, 1806	Christian Haun—Nancy Froter		
Feb. 5, 1807	Samuel Hill—Jane Culbertson		
Feb. 19, 1807	Jesse Starnes—Rosanna Brown		
Mar. 26, 1807	Amos Ryon—Patsy Horton		
May 27, 1807	James Penny—Polly Gann		Adam Gann
June 27, 1807	Benson Hunt—Mary Magdalene Pope		John Hunt
June 27, 1807	John Keener—Rebecca Odle		Jesse Viney
July 1, 1807	William McCray—Maria Koontz		
July 15, 1807	William Felts—Peggy Lacky		
July 20, 1807	Reuben Burk—Lacy Forbes		Thomas Carbury
July 25, 1807	Levi Fisher—Elizabeth Reed		L. Hundley
Aug. 6, 1807	Davis Smith—Latty Hombarger		
Aug. 7, 1807	James Rigsby—Mapy Gittson		Thomas Rigsby
Aug. 12, 1807	William Thresher—Elizabeth Kennedy		
			Joseph Hartman
Aug. 17, 1807	William Lovelace—Rebecca Hawkins		
Sept. 7, 1807	John Wortman—Elizabeth Thompson		Robert Dennis
Oct. 9, 1807	Joseph Mauk—Grace Broyles		Simon Broyles

Date	Male	Female	Bondman
Oct. 11, 1807	Greenbury Boren—Mary Ruble		Benjamin Miller
Oct. 12, 1807	Robert Chapman—Anna Martin		John Chapman
Nov. 15, 1807	James Baird—Edy Nelson		Singleton Pritchett
Nov. 25, 1807	John Tittle—Jain Rigsby		Acy Rigsby
Feb. 25, 1808	Jacob Miller—Sarah Nole		
Feb. 26, 1808	Daniel Wright—Phebe Porter		Lindsay Rit
Feb. 29, 1808	William Stephens—Elizabeth Melvin		Mark Mears
Mar. 10, 1808	William McGinnis—Millie Conley		
Mar. 28, 1808	John Jones—Sarah Daniels		
Mar. 31, 1808	John Anderson—Margaret Christian		
June 7, 1808	Henry Short—Jane Miller		
June 27, 1808	Reuben Bayles—Elizabeth Moore		Henry McCray
July 28, 1808	Robert McClure—Margaret Thompson		
Aug. 20, 1808	Henry McPherson—Sussanah Glasscock		
Aug. 29, 1808	Thomas Murray—Peggy Messer		
Oct. 5, 1808	Rheuben Bayles, Jr.—Sarah Young		Joseph Young
Oct. 12, 1808	Michael Sands—Elizabeth Gardner		
Oct. 12, 1808	David Luster—Sarah Garland		
Oct. 12, 1808	James Arrington—Patsy Bell		
Dec. 30, 1808	James Beckham—Sarah Glass		
Feb. 7, 1809	John Massengail—Margaret Broyles		Daniel Broyles
Feb. 21, 1809	Turner Smith—Mary Ruble		
Feb. 22, 1809	Horatis Baldwin—Polly Whitakre		
Mar. 8, 1809	Joseph Duncan—Rhoda Hunt		George Wallace
Mar. 30, 1809	John Carriger—Margaret Elliot		
April 14, 1809	Edmund Waren—Jenny Baker		
April 22, 1809	John McCardell—Sara Phillips		
May 16, 1809	David Mitchell—Jane McClure		
June 11, 1809	Benjamin Worham—Rebeccah Johnston		
June 26, 1809	William Barnes—Mary Blair		
June 28, 1809	John Gann—Rebeccah Massengail		David Brumley
July 27, 1809	Thomas Smalling—Rachel Smith		Jaramyah Smith
Aug. 15, 1809	William Duncan—Ruth Odell		Jesse Hampton
Oct. 11, 1809	Larrence Glase—Hanah Humphres		Robert McFarling
Oct. 22, 1809	Joseph C. Bell—Nancy White		
Oct. 24, 1809	Joseph Ball—Nancy Brown		
Nov. 25, 1809	Jesse Clark—Agnes Williams		Barnes Clark
Jan. 1, 1810	Samuel Davis—Sarah Letsinger		
Jan. 2, 1810	Jacob Million—Mary May		
Jan. 15, 1810	William Dykes—Ginny Mare		
Jan. 20, 1810	John Booth, Jr.—Sally Rodgers		Samuel Cloyd
Jan. 30, 1810	John Cox—Priscilla Templin		
Feb. 20, 1810	Samuel Ball—Mary Cole		

Date	Male	Female	Bondman
Mar. 14, 1810	Frederick Starnes—Elizabeth Soltz		
May 25, 1810	Jacob Miller—Margaret Kelley		
July 9, 1810	William Brittan—Sally Smith		
Sept. 10, 1810	Moses Hutchins—Polly Carder		John Clouse
Sept. 17, 1810	Walter Emerson—Albina R. Cassen		
Sept. 23, 1810	Zeadox Freman—Hannah Grayham		Wm. Grayham
Oct. 16, 1810	Isaac Horton—Margaret Martin		Thomas Collier
Oct. 18, 1810	Alexander Campbell—Polly Strain		Robert Strain
Oct. 27, 1810	Horation Ford, Jr.—Jane Careathers		John Mallonee
Nov. 12, 1810	Jacob Poland—Sarah Couch		Elijah Crouch
Dec. 4, 1810	Martin Click—Betsy Martin		Charles Grimes
Dec. 18, 1810	John Bass—Rebecca Horton		Jesse Mullins
Dec. 19, 1810	Joshua Green—Susannah Greenway		John Mathes
Dec. 26, 1810	Wyland Barger—Christina Cilty		Henry Barger
Dec. 26, 1810	Samuel Erwin—Mary Tilson		
Jan. 2, 1811	James Price—Frances Threewitts		John C. Harris
Jan. 4, 1811	Adam Clause—Elizabeth Hutskins		
Jan. 5, 1811	Emanuel Good—Nancy Rymill		John McNeal
Jan. 5, 1811	David Good—Sarah Hartsell		Joseph Mock
Jan. 19, 1811	Jacob Headrick—Betsy Mygiar		Samuel Early
Jan. 22, 1811	John Blair—Peggy McCall		
Jan. 25, 1811	John McClure—Sarah Million		
Jan. 28, 1811	Jacob Cosner—Peggy Delany		Jacob Miller
Jan. 28, 1811	William Kindel—Caty May		John Clingman
Feb. 4, 1811	William Roberts—Eve Ruble		Jacob Gyer
Feb. 11, 1811	Robert Chester—Martha Jones		John Chester
Feb. 16, 1811	Samuel Yearly—Delilah Hartsil		Reuben Wilhite
Feb. 27, 1811	John Matthews—Rosannah Blackburn		John Nelson
Feb. 28, 1811	Grant Ford—Nacky Ford		James Ford
Mar. 7, 1811	Pleasant Wallace—Anne Gann		John Marcer
Mar. 8, 1811	Jeremiah Boyd—Susannah Ryker		George Chandler
Mar. 11, 1811	Stephen Brown—Betsy Tucker		Abraham Brown
Mar. 21, 1811	Jacob Brown—Sally Million		Isaac Brown
April 4, 1811	John Clinger—Betsy Rymill		William Gann
April 13, 1811	Edmend Hodge—Susannah Dunkin		James Haws
April 13, 1811	James Black—Rachel Spring		John Patton
May 9, 1811	Robert Faubush—Elizabeth Hinkle		Thomas Faubush
May 14, 1811	Thomas Allman—Sarah Huffman		William Templin
June 12, 1811	Abraham Britten—Nancy Brannon		Richard Kean
June 19, 1811	David McGinnis—Sarah White		
June 19, 1811	William Isler—Polly Spring		Jacob Overholser
June 28, 1811	James Jones—Hannah Maiden		John Burtch
June 29, 1811	Ransom Medlock—Barbara Hail		Richard Kean

Date	Male	Female	Bondman
July 20, 1811	James Chandle—Barbara Kike		Jeremiah Boyd
July 25, 1811	Henry McKraken—Nancy Barclay		
Aug. 1, 1811	William Murray—Elizabeth Miller		Abraham Tipton
Aug. 8, 1811	William Huston—Jane Jenkins		Benjamin Renno
Aug. 9, 1811	Jacob Mock—Margaret Hemp		Joseph Mock
Aug. 12, 1811	Israel Poulston—Betsy Pitcocke		
Aug. 29, 1811	Abijah Sands—Polly Shields		William Carmickael
Sept. 1, 1811	Thomas Hunt—Martina Bayles		
Sept. 7, 1811	Samuel Miller—Artey Bean		John Bean
Sept. 10, 1811	William Crawford—Martha Ford		Charles Denham
Sept. 27, 1811	Andrew Graham—Ruth Carson		John Carson
Oct. 7, 1811	Peter Vandeventer—Mary Casner		Jacob McCoy
Oct. 7, 1811	Robert Taylor—Hannah Sands		Isaac Sands
Oct. 22, 1811	William Jones—Elizabeth Clouse		
Nov. 4, 1811	John Basket—Tiney Taylor		
Dec. 4, 1811	Clark Ellis—Nancy Lekins		
Dec. 18, 1811	William McJimsey—Nancy Brown		Jesse Brown
Dec. 23, 1811	Adam Broyles—Polly Walker		John Laman
Dec. 25, 1811	Hezekiah Bayles—Mary Finch		
Dec. 26, 1811	John Carson—Hannah Carson		
Jan. ....., 1812	Jesse Lunsford—Rebecca Peterson		
Jan. 15, 1812	William Patton—Jane Hannah		
Feb. 14, 1812	Isaac Sands—Betsy Benner		Archibald Fream
Feb. 15, 1812	William F. King—Ruth Little		
Feb. 16, 1812	Joseph Williams—Nancy Collier		
Feb. 27, 1812	John Hodge—Mary Acuff		Thompson Henry
Feb. 29, 1812	Thomas Ford—Isbel Carethers		Micajah Ford
Mar. 16, 1812	Ezekiel Chanler—Sussannah Chanler		Joseph Chanler
Mar. 28, 1812	William Jones—Nancy Koon		Darling Jones
April 9, 1812	David Painter—Rebecca Car		William Painter
April 14, 1812	Micajah Ford—Ann Briant		
April 16, 1812	John Conkin—Polly Jackson		George Conkin
April 27, 1812	William Delany—Elizabeth Goins		Amon Boring
April 29, 1812	John Fannen—Polly Hinch		
May 5, 1812	Daniel Denton—Susannah White		
May 10, 1812	Jacob Billingsley—Rebecca Shipley		James Billingsley
May 29, 1812	Mathew Douglas—Nancy King		
June 9, 1812	Morgan Murray—Sarah Ford		Murry King
June 22, 1812	Thomas Price—Margaret Harrison		Amon Boring
July 25, 1812	Hezekiah Boring—Polly Melvin		
July 25, 1812	Johnny Bacon—Dorcas Jackson		
Aug. 22, 1812	Jacob Skipper—Nancy Magee		Henry Fergeson
Aug. 27, 1812	Isaac Floyd—Margaret Thorp		Moses Humphreys

Date	Male	Female	Bondman
Sept. 18, 1812	Thomas Ford—Margaret Chapman		Ezekiel Wright
Sept. 24, 1812	David Russell—Jane Stuart		
Sept. 26, 1812	Joseph Bell—Sarah Clark		John C. Harris
Sept. 29, 1812	John Tadlock—Polly Morton		Jesse Mullin
Oct. 14, 1812	Daniel McKay—Polly Prichard		
Oct. 29, 1812	Jacob Kebler—Polly Haws		James Keebler
Oct. 31, 1812	John Whitlock—Marcia Mullinaux		William Grimsley
Nov. 8, 1812	Jesse Bacon—Elizabeth Pritchard		Jeremiah Bacon
Nov. 14, 1812	Reuben Rogers—Bethsheba Haile		J. C. Harris
Dec. 1, 1812	John Gann—Sally Painter		Daniel Gann
Dec. 17, 1812	Levi Beals—Malinda Wyington		Ezekeil Lyon
Dec. 23, 1812	Isaac McCardle—Jane Morrison		Phillip McCardell
Jan. 12, 1813	David McNabb—Peggy Whitson		
Jan. 16, 1813	John Ruble—Caty Slagle		
Jan. 27, 1813	John Stevens—Margaret Duncan		David Stevens
Jan. 28, 1813	James McCarroll—Sarah Forbush		Henry Forguson
Feb. 23, 1813	John France—Betsy Burris		John Scott
Mar. 3, 1813	Samuel Sherfey—Betsy Goodman		James Acton
April 7, 1813	David G. McCarty—Elizabeth Starns		
April 6, 1813	Hugh Weir—Sally Duncan		Robert Gray
May 8, 1813	David Stanfield—Betsy Bailes		Levi Beals
May 11, 1813	Adonis May—Betsy McGinnis		John McGinnis
May 12, 1813	George Jackson—Nancy Bacon		
May 13, 1813	Shepherd Irwin—Matilda Ann Dunham		
			John Phillips
May 30, 1813	Nicholas Reasoner—Polly Miller		Jacob Miller
June 17, 1813	Michael H. Martin—Polly Tadlock		Thomas Eakin
June 29, 1813	Charley Lemmon—Eve Tossen		
July 10, 1813	Gabriel Morgan—Mary Whitlock		J. C. Harris
July 26, 1813	Joseph Crouch—Polly Hanley		Thomas Whitson
July 27, 1813	Jesse Riggs—Mary Ann Barron		Jehu Ford
July 27, 1813	Elizah Bigs—Mary Ann Baum		
Aug. 6, 1813	Bartlett H. Odle—Elizabeth Quillin		Joseph Kiener
Aug. 7, 1813	John Sherffey—Magdeleny Coffman		
Aug. 12, 1813	William Bailes—Rachel Squibb		Caleb Squibb
Aug. 17, 1813	Joseph Lane—Mary L. Campbell		
			Alexander Campbell
Sept. 4, 1813	Matthias Keen—Rachel Brown		Elijah Keen
Sept. 30, 1813	William Grimsley—Esthe Wheelock		Richard White
Oct. 13, 1813	John McCorkle—Polly Cunningham		Robert Baker
Nov. 4, 1813	William Wheeler, Jr.—Elizabeth Little		Reece Tipton
Nov. 15, 1813	George Masingill—Hanna Jones		Monty Stuart
Dec. 20, 1813	Abraham Brown—Nancy Wiggins		William Bayles

Date	Male	Female	Bondman
Dec. 22, 1813	James Depew—Susannah Cox		L. Anderson
Dec. 23, 1813	Adam Massy—Diniah Smith		
Jan. 9, 1814	Robert W. Strain—Nancy Biddle		Samuel Biddle
Feb. 2, 1814	Jacob White—Nancy Carbury		David McGinnis
Feb. 3, 1814	Joseph Parker Baggatt—Mary Lansdown		
Feb. 7, 1814	Joseph Crouch—Betsy Keyfauver		John Bean
Feb. 7, 1814	Abraham Tipton—Polly Boring		Francis Willett
Feb. 19, 1814	Thomas Nelson—Delilah Mayfield		Samuel Mirault
Feb. 27, 1814	Charles Dunworth—Elizabeth Melvin		Thomas Bacon
Mar. 10, 1814	Joseph Brown—Lydia Hammonds		
Mar. 24, 1814	Benjamin Gray—Matilda Lackens		
April 21, 1814	Anthony Holland—Barbara Cutzilus		
May 12, 1814	Joseph Brummet—Patsy Cassady		
May 21, 1814	John Harvey—Jane Elliott		
June 2, 1814	Reuben Gann—Eliza Clark		Pleasant Wallace
June 14, 1814	Davis—Patsy Bennet		Jacob Hartsell
July 25, 1814	Thomas Thacker—Mary Byerly		Michael Byerly
Aug. 9, 1814	John Cole—Catherine Layman		
Aug. 12, 1814	Joseph Smith—Sarah Brown		
Aug. 18, 1814	Jacob McCordle—Rebecca Ball		Philip McCordle
Aug. 20, 1814	Elizah Brown—Polly Glass		John McKeakin
Sept. 1, 1814	David Stevens—Lurena Duncan		Isaac Little
Sept. 7, 1814	Pointon Charlton—Rachel McLin		James Given
Sept. 10, 1814	Enoch Jobe—Elizabeth Jackson		Thomas Haile
Sept. 10, 1814	William Crawford—Martha Ford		
Sept. 11, 1814	Francis Register—Jeremiah Glascock		
Dec. 3, 1814	Thomas Douglass—Nancy Barron		
....., 1815	Joseph B. Bacon—		James Givin
....., 1815	William Carmichael—Patsey Blair		Arche Carmichael
Jan. 4, 1815	Abraham Fine—Margaret Lusser		
Jan. 5, 1815	William Mahoney—Betsy Pardue		
Jan. 31, 1815	John Blair—Levica Shields		
Mar. 22, 1815	Daniel Perkons—Betsy Beard		
April 13, 1815	Jacob Hoss—Margaret Bean		
May 11, 1815	David Bowman—Sally Smith		
May 18, 1815	Michael Byerly—Patsy Thacker		
May 23, 1815	William Crouch—Sam Hunt		
May 27, 1815	William Keen—Betsy Taylor		
June 1, 1815	James Henry—Sarah Murry		Baxter Bean
June 19, 1815	Charles Beane—Margaret Cloyd		Christen Sliger
June 20, 1815	Henry Carrell—Ann Strain		Eli Richey
June 20, 1815	Joseph Clark—Polly Basket		
June 20, 1815	Caleb Martin—Sally Bird		Peter Gardner

Date	Male	Female	Bondman
June 23, 1815	Thomas Biddill—Betsy Blair		Samuel Biddel
July 3, 1815	John Holleby—Phebe Brown		William White
July 27, 1814	Jacob Rymal—Francis Broyles		
July 8, 1815	Joseph Star—Susannah Williams		Michael Stair
July 8, 1815	David Rice—Jane R. Doak		David Deaderick
Aug. 4, 1815	Elijah Kelby—Elizabeth Briant		John G. Rubel
Aug. 10, 1815	Sammie Lane—Mary Humphries		
Aug. 11, 1815	Jacob Watenburger—Hannah Citty		
Aug. 15, 1815	Chaise Hail—Clary Kinchels		Baxter Bean
Aug. 31, 1815	John Patton—Susannah Broyles		
Sept. 5, 1815	John Marr—Patience Tucker		
Sept. 5, 1815	Dancy Price—Mary Swonger		
Sept. 11, 1815	Samuel Chapman—Rachael Basket		Benj. Chapman
Sept. 17, 1815	John Ingle—Barbara Ingle		
Sept. 20, 1815	Abraham Moore—Polly Morgan		William Grimsley
Sept. 23, 1815	John Peter French—Eliza Hartman		
Sept. 28, 1815	David Rogers—Martha Young		Thomas Rogers
Oct. 2, 1815	Lewis Broiles—Elizabeth Calvert		Thomas Finch
Oct. 4, 1815	James Caruthers—Orpha Huston		
Oct. 7, 1815	Jacob Davott—Polly Hodge		Martin Kitzmiler
Oct. 10, 1815	George White—Sally Nelson		David McGinnis
Oct. 12, 1815	Burridge Brannon—Polly Cassady		Josiah Tucker
Oct. 13, 1815	William Parker—Mary Ensor		William S. Parker
Oct. 20, 1815	Sherword Vaughn—Elizabeth Hale		John McCracken
Nov. 1, 1815	Alexander Fulkerson—Deborah Jackson		
			George Jackson
Nov. 4, 1815	James Crawford—Elizabeth Wheeler		Lewis Wheeler
Nov. 14, 1815	Joseph McCorkel—Mary Hendry		
Nov. 30, 1815	Jeramiah Rogers—Sarah Springs		
Nov. 30, 1815	William B. Carter—Eliza M. Aiken		
Dec. 20, 1815	Elijah Rogers—Barthena Sargent		Isaac Hair
Dec. 23, 1815	Elijah Brown—Betsy Glass		James Givin
Dec. 24, 1815	Joseph Hale—Ibby McAdams		
Dec. 24, 1815	Andrew Baker—Nancy Briant		
Dec. 26, 1815	Robert McCall—Jemima Wilson		Uriah Hunt
......, 1816	Henry McCracken—Katherine Hamilton		
Jan. 1, 1816	John Rankin—Jane Lowry		
Jan 2, 1816	Thomas Whitson—Susannah Willett		
			Jonathan Mulkey
Jan. 17, 1816	Eli Richey—Nancy Duncan		Nat'l. Jones
Jan. 18, 1816	Thomas Arrington—Sebitha Bell		
Jan. 23, 1816	Jacob Brown—Polly Salts		
Jan. 31, 1816	Joshua S. Hail—Ruth Hail		Nicholas Chineth

Date	Male	Female	Bondman
Feb. 8, 1816	John Depew—Catherine Bacon	James Depew
Feb. 14, 1816	William Miller—Betsy Rebecca Arrerwood	William Irwin
Feb. 15, 1816	Samuel Jackson—Catharine Bacon	George Jackson
Feb. 22, 1816	Ezekial Stanbury—Sarah Grayham	Charles Graham
Feb. 27, 1816	Daniel Gray—Isabella Mitchell	
Mar. 21, 1816	Jacob Bull—Nancy Hazlett	
April 16, 1816	Covington Collingsworth—Elizabeth Shipley	James Ellis
April 24, 1816	David A. Deaderick—Adelaide Eliza Jackson	
April 27, 1816	Elijah Keen—Ann White	Jonas Keen
April 30, 1816	John Nelson, Jr.—Minerva G. Sevier	
May 12, 1816	James Hail—Jane Gray	
May 24, 1816	James Jones—Martha Hern	
June 19, 1816	Robert McLin—Ann Blair	Sam'l W. Doak
June 20, 1816	David Star—Betsy Combs	John Star
June 23, 1816	Robert Beard—Sarah Glasscock	John Miller
July 3, 1816	John Loyd—Betsy Depew	David Nelson
July 4, 1816	Wesley Owen—Elizabeth Winchester	David Stuart
July 13, 1816	Isaac B. McClellan—Margaret R. Greer	
July 15, 1816	William Williams—Sally Wilhite	
July 18, 1816	Frederick S. Heiskell—Elizabeth Brown	
July 24, 1816	Smith Hunt—Patsey Alison	James Davis
July 31, 1816	Jonathan Douglass—Jane Young	
Aug. 7, 1816	Nathaniel Hall—Lucinda Hail	Shadrack Hail
Aug. 11, 1816	John Rineheart—Jane Medlock	William T. Ensor
Aug. 14, 1816	Isaac Haire—Sally Russell	James Adair, Jr.
Aug. 15, 1816	Charles Whitson—Nancy Dunkin	James Guinn
Aug. 27, 1816	Joseph McGinnis—Peggy Faubush	John Cox
Aug. 29, 1816	John Adwell—Mary Hale	Nathan Job
Sept. 12, 1816	Joshua Miller—Elizabeth Bull	Elisha Bull
Sept. 23, 1816	Ladox Freeman—Hannah Grayham	
Sept. 26, 1816	Nelson Mitchell—Betsy Fawbush	Geo. C. Harris
Oct. 2, 1816	Sample Orr—Hester Salts	
Oct. 8, 1816	William Brown—Savannah Nelson	
Oct. 9, 1816	Richard Silcock—Polly Aker	
Oct. 9, 1816	Jacob Roller—Rebecca Lartz	
Oct. 14, 1816	John Baxter—Nancy Peeples	Benjamin Rector
Oct. 15, 1816	John Cooper—Susannah Giger	
Oct. 19, 1816	Benjamin Epperson—Nancy Barnon (or Barron)	
Oct. 24, 1816	John Donald—Polly Kein	Nathan Shipley
Nav. 4, 1816	Adam Shanks—Susannah Sharfey	
Nov. 7, 1816	Elisha Bull—Sarah Davis	Jesse Bull

Date	Male	Female	Bondman
Nov. 7, 1816	John B. Ellis—Rebecca Trivathan		
Nov. 10, 1816	Walter Hale—Nancy Smith		
Nov. 19, 1816	Jesse Bayless—Nancy Shanon	Peter Miller	
Nov. 20, 1816	John Morrison—Thankful Morrison	John Merida	
Nov. 22, 1816	John Webb—Nancy Clouse	Nathan Peeples	
Nov. 28, 1816	Samuel Keesler—Catherine Bowman		
Dec. 17, 1816	Samuel Erwin—Mercy Tilson	William Irwin	
Dec. 19, 1816	William Brit—Nancy Waller	Benjamin Brit	
Dec. 19, 1816	Henry Nash—Mary Ann Shields		
Dec. 21, 1816	John V. Hoss—Nancy Basket	Peter Miller	
Dec. 24, 1816	Andrew Baker—Nancy Briant	Elisha McCray	
Dec. 31, 1816	Charles Brannen—Maria Engle		
Jan. 2, 1817	Mardicai Price—Anes Thompson		
Jan. 7, 1817	John W. Brown—Margaret Kincheloe	Joshua Hale	
Jan. 27, 1817	William Anderson—Hester Russell		
Jan. 29, 1817	Joshua Hail—Polly Glascock		
Feb. 1, 1817	Alexander McGinty—Elizabeth Ruble		
Feb. 2, 1817	John McGee—Sarah Snapp		
Feb. 8, 1817	John Star—Sarah Combs	Jonathan Baker	
Feb. 14, 1817	Philip Bowlin—Catherine Walters	William Bottles	
Feb. 16, 1817	John Lowdy—Polly Wheeler	William Wheeler	
Feb. 20, 1817	Thomas May—Peggy Spore	William Wilson	
Feb. 25, 1817	John Hunter—Polly Brown		
Feb. 27, 1817	William Nelson—Sally Critzelus	George White	
Feb. 27, 1817	Jacob Range—Susanna Hail	Peter Miller, Jr.	
Feb. 26, 1817	Wilton M. Atkinson—Martha B. Macken		
Mar. 2, 1817	William Lisenby—Isbel Young		
Mar. 6, 1817	William Starnes—Sally Holly	William Graham	
Mar. 10, 1817	William Shields—Eliza Conway		
Mar. 13, 1817	John McCall—Polly Martin	John Blair	
Mar. 13, 1817	George Bayles—Nancy Goforth	Daniel Bayles	
Mar. 17, 1817	George Smith—Ruth Smith	Jeremiah D. Smith	
Mar. 19, 1817	Moses Nelson—Hannah Gann		
Mar. 26, 1817	Andrew Duncan—Margaret R. Alexander	Hugh Wear	
Mar. 28, 1817	Jeremiah D. Gibson—Phebe Jobe		
April 3, 1817	Andrew Duncan—Ann Carson		
April 8, 1817	Henry Deakins—Rosannah Burris		
May 20, 1817	Samuel Lemmon—Lydia Boothe	Emanuel Lamons	
May 22, 1817	Abraham Lysenby—Rebecca Simpson		
May 27, 1817	John Slagle—Elizabeth Delany		
June 7, 1817	Macajah Elherton—Rachel Farlan		
June 26, 1817	William White—Jane Mitchell	Adam White	
June 29, 1817	Henry Hale—Harriet Kincheloe	William Brown	

14

Date	Male	Female	Bondman
June 30, 1817	David Mitchell—Polly Cowpenger		Robert Church
July 4, 1817	William Justice—Nelly McColip		Sam Bayles
July 21, 1817	Joseph Woods—Catherine Grayham		
July 22, 1817	Jacob Shanks—Mary Isenburg		Abraham Tipton
July 23, 1817	John Hulmer—Elizabeth White		
July 31, 1817	James Williams—Katharine Jones		James Gwin
Aug. 5, 1817	Robert Henry—Hannah Whitehead		Joseph Nelson
Aug. 12, 1817	John Hurian—Sarah Miller		
Aug. 17, 1817	Isaac Range—Elizabeth Humphreys		
Aug. 20, 1817	John Cox—Ruth Gray		Thomas Hail
Aug. 27, 1817	Peter Miller—Polly Hunt		
Sept. 4, 1817	John King—Sarah White		Adam White
Sept. 11, 1817	Thomas Messer—Elizabeth Geruin (or Gwin)		
Sept. 21, 1817	Tobias Speck—Hannah McCordle		
Oct. 9, 1817	Adam Ingle—Elizabeth Sliger		Alexander Mathes
Oct. 11, 1817	Thomas Davis—Sally Moore		
Oct. 12, 1817	Christopher Long—Sarah Sliger		
Oct. 12, 1817	Emanuel Love—Polly Sliger		
Oct. 12, 1817	Daniel Salts—Rebecca McCardle		
Oct. 23, 1817	Richard Grier—Martha Gray		Abraham Haun
Oct. 27, 1817	Richard Vaughn—Frances Robertson		Robert Phurr
Nov. 30, 1817	Jonathin Collins—Jane Bolin		
Dec. 4, 1817	Isaac Ford—Caty Mowl		William Keloner
Dec. 11, 1817	A. Geahl—Christina Snapp		
Dec. 12, 1817	George Ricard—Jemina Ellis		Joseph McCleary
Dec. 23, 1817	Jacob Clipper—Catharine Bowman		
Dec. 23, 1817	John Ryland—Hannah Brown		John Blair
Dec. 25, 1817	George Haile—Nancy Shipley		
Dec. 25, 1817	Anthony Russell—Sarah Harris		
Dec. 29, 1817	Henry French—Catharine Watson		Dafid Cannon
Dec. ...., 1817	John Wright—Barbara Range		W. B. Carter
Jan. 14, 1818	Daniel McCray—Sarah Bogart		
Jan. 16, 1818	John Ruble—Caty Slagle		Turner Smith
Jan. 30, 1818	Micajah Hodges—Elizabeth Gray		Maiden George
Jan. 16, 1818	Joseph Melvin—Sarah Delany		
Jan. 15, 1818	Levi Archer—Rachel Archer		Joseph Archer
Jan. 29, 1818	Berges Barckley—Elizabeth Barckley		
Feb. 11, 1818	Baty Philips—Phebe Bayles		William Tyler
Feb. 21, 1818	John Gann—Juda Frazier		
Mar. 3, 1818	Jonathan Mulkey, Sr.—Anna Lacy		
Mar. 12, 1818	Robert Bean—Caty Sliger		
Mar. 24, 1818	George Barnes—Jemima Jackson		
Mar. 25, 1818	John Smith—Martha Blair		

Date	Male	Female	Bondman
Mar. 26, 1818	Edward Stanbury—Polly Ann Graham		
Mar. 28, 1818	Isaac Cox—Sarah Lessenbery		
April 14, 1818	Enoch Wheelock—Lucy Irwin		
May 7, 1818	Adam G. Dean—Nancy Miller		
May 8, 1818	Thomas P. Ensor—Hannah Jobe		
May 19, 1818	James Fuller—Tabitha Denton		
May 19, 1818	Samuel Bogart—Rachel Hammer		
June 20, 1818	Ezra Chester—Nancy Hale		John Chester
July 5, 1818	Samuel Dugles—Elizabeth Bacon		
July 30, 1818	Joseph Chinnoth—Liddy Bean		Joshua S. Hale
July 21, 1818	John Wallace—Elizabeth Messer		Joseph Merser
Aug. 8, 1818	John Summerman—Magdalean Coughfman		
Sept. 8, 1818	John Howser—Margaret Rutlet		
Sept. 15, 1818	Robert McClure—Rebecca Mathews		David Mitchell
Oct. 1, 1818	Edward L. Martan—Mariah Bartly		
Oct. 4, 1818	Mathew Salts—Nancy Beavers		
Oct. 18, 1818	James Cronell—Letty Tapp		
Oct. 21, 1818	James Fullen—Malinda Broyles		
Oct. 25, 1818	John Wolf—Anny McKihen		
Oct. 29, 1818	Daniel Barnes—Polly Bacon		
Nov. 2, 1818	George Reeder—James Sherrill		
Nov. 2, 1818	John Crouch—Nancy Epperson		
Nov. 11, 1818	Samuel Wright—Sarah Price		
Nov. 17, 1818	John Lackey—Mary Rollins		
Nov. 23, 1818	Robert Allison—Elleanor Hodges		
Nov. 26, 1818	Richard B. Purden—Susan B. Sevier		
Dec. 4, 1818	Barnibas May—Margaret Ruble		
Dec. 22, 1818	Alexander Campbell—Nelly Brown		
Dec. 24, 1818	John Mitchell—Elizabeth Coppinger		
Dec. 25, 1818	Isaac Martin—Polly Ellis		
Dec. 25, 1818	Anthony Pate—Elizabeth Lain		
Dec. 26, 1818	Brooksey H. Bell—Elizabeth Broyles		
Dec. 26, 1818	William Baker—Betsy Lott		
Jan. 7, 1819	Samuel Devault—Patty Crouch		
Jan. 8, 1819	John Mitchell—Sarah Salts		
Jan. 14, 1819	Royal Phillips—Jane Bacon		
Jan. 18, 1819	James Lewis—Lucy Holt		
Jan. 24, 1819	Zachariah Shields—Nancy Sullins		
Jan. 26, 1819	Henry Hair—Elizabeth Taylor		
Jan. 28, 1819	John Miller, Jr.—Mary Kelly		
Feb. 3, 1819	John Clipper—Susannah Bowman		
Feb. 3, 1819	Charles Deakins—Rachel Nelson		
Feb. 4, 1819	William King—Sarah Hale		

Date	Male	Female	Bondman
Feb. 4, 1819	James Johnson—Cristina Brown		
Feb. 4, 1819	Samuel Houston—Mrs. Isabella Gray		
Feb. 11, 1819	Jacob Boring—Alice Green		
Feb. 15, 1819	James Fulkerson—Elizabeth Waddle		
Feb. 16, 1819	Philip Emert—Deby Lyons		
Mar. 2, 1819	George Fulk—Sentry Leonard		
Mar. 9, 1819	Peter Watleberger—Margaret Slyger		
Mar. 16, 1819	John Billingly—Polly Hale		
April 9, 1819	Daniel Isenbarg—Lidia Moler		
April 11, 1819	William Rikert—Susannah Moler		
April 12, 1819	Pointon Charlton—Rebeckah Miller		
May 6, 1819	Henry M. Helvin—Nancy Shanklin		
May 29, 1819	John Gibson—Catherine Vaugn		
June 3, 1819	William P. Kenner—Elizabeth White		
June 9, 1819	Isaac Elsey—Ina Cone		
June 15, 1819	James Simpson—Polly Hammer		
July 1, 1819	Enoch Shipley—Elizabeth Hoss		
July 15, 1819	Fleming B. Evans—Margaret Atkinson		
July 18, 1819	John Koonts—Sarah Delashmont		
July 19, 1819	David Ludon—Alley Bird		
July 20, 1819	Sam Randolph—Ann Bayless		
July 21, 1819	Jater Hicks—Julia D. Nelson		
July 22, 1819	John Layman—Elizabeth Coughman		
Aug. 1, 1819	John Rhea—Elizabeth Blevin		
Aug. 2, 1819	William King—Patsy Crouch		Nathan Gregg
Aug. 9, 1819	Thomas Brown—Sarah McCray		
Aug. 15, 1819	Duglas Dinkens—Sary Braden		
Aug. 17, 1819	John Arthurburn—Nancy Billingsley		
Aug. 18, 1819	Benjamin Croggins—Margaret Starnes		
Aug. 21, 1819	Isaac E. W. Bacon—Sarah Hunt		
Aug. 24, 1819	John Chaney—Mary Fulman		
Sept. 3, 1819	Andrew Lilburn—Eafy Walker		
Sept. 8, 1819	Joseph Nelson—Elizabeth Gilmore		
Sept. 28, 1819	Samuel R. Brown—Nancy Balah		
Sept. 29, 1819	John Bovell—Christiana Gray		
Oct. 7, 1819	Isaac Richards—Peggy Snapp		
Oct. 9, 1819	Manley McNabb—Polly Faubush		
Oct. 10, 1819	Isaac Cox—Mary Hellin		
Oct. 14, 1819	Henderson Clark—Ann West		
Oct. 20, 1819	John Hammer—Martha White		
Oct. 20, 1819	John Kannon—Elizabeth Freeman		
Oct. 21, 1819	Westley Earnest—Mary Payne		
Oct. 21, 1819	James Green—Priscilla Hunter		

Date	Male	Female	Bondman
Nov. 3, 1819	John Worley—Sarah Range		
Nov. 8, 1819	John Bayles—Elizabeth Bacon		
Nov. 11, 1819	James Bell—Sarah Anders		
Nov. 17, 1819	Oulen Roberts—Jain Mitchell		
Dec. 2, 1819	John Ryland—Rebeckah Liking		
Dec. 6, 1819	Daniel Linebaugh—Nancy McCollum		Robert Taylor
Dec. 23, 1819	James Dotson—Elizabeth Overholser		
Dec. 25, 1819	William Odell—Margaret Sailor		
Dec. 29, 1819	Samuel Biddle—Margaret Wilson		
Dec. 30, 1819	David Britt—Annah Harmon		
Jan. 5, 1820	William Egeman—Lucinda King		
Jan. 15, 1820	John Cassidy—Elizabeth Brummitt		
Jan. 21, 1820	Joseph Howard—Rachel Rector		
Feb. 3, 1820	David Robinson—Nancy Jenkins		
Feb. 16, 1820	Oliver B. Ross—Harriet Jackson		
Feb. 24, 1820	James White—Peggy Bayles		
Feb. 25, 1820	Samuel Byerly—Elizabeth Williams		
Mar. 7, 1820	Eli Kean—Nancy Barren		Jesse Riggs
Mar. 8, 1820	Thomas White—Jane Young		
Mar. 19, 1820	Ephriam France—Anne Andes		
Mar. 23, 1820	Leon Price—Polly Brown		
Mar. 23, 1820	James Harvey—Armacy Clark		
April 2, 1820	Joseph Marshall—Mary Hoss		
April 4, 1820	John Crouch—Elizabeth Jenkins		
April 11, 1820	Timothy Burress—Susan Norris		
April 19, 1820	Enoch Hale—Pheby Haws		
May 10, 1820	Moses Bunker—Eliza Graham		
May 24, 1820	John Miller—Catherine Good		
May 28, 1820	John Ruble—Catherine Coon		
June 25, 1820	John Bacon—Leigh Jackson		
July 11, 1820	Henry Fon—Sarah Isenbarger		
July 15, 1820	Westley Hunt—Margaret Patton		
July 29, 1820	Conrad Coughman—Ann Philip		
July 31, 1820	John Bowman—Polly Duncan		
Aug. 3, 1820	George Murr—Catherine Hummond		
Aug. 4, 1820	Peter Jackson—Ann Murray		
Aug. 6, 1820	Roderick Shelton—Rachel Moore		
Aug. 24, 1820	Solomon Crown—Susan Bowman		
Aug. 24, 1820	Daniel Wetheford—Catherine Leaman		
Aug. 28, 1820	James Norris—Mary Brummit		
Aug. 30, 1820	Joshua Swanger—Nancy Howard		Daniel Francis
Aug. 30, 1820	John P. Lessenberg—Elizabeth Reeves		
Sept. 1, 1820	John Green—Margaret Shields		

Date	Male	Female	Bondman
Sept. 11, 1820	John L. Williams—Elizabeth Price		
Sept. 14, 1820	William B. Stackhouse—Jane McNabb		
Oct. 11, 1820	William Bottles—P. Mary Hammonds		
Oct. 16, 1820	Henry Miller—Jane Young		
Oct. 16, 1820	Lewis Lisenby—Nancy Faubush		
Oct. 18, 1820	Lewallen King—Susannah Crouch		
Nov. 9, 1820	John S. Bails—Elizabeth Nelson		
Nov. 14, 1820	William Dosser—Malinda Rogan		
Dec. 4, 1820	Henry Luntsford—Alsey Hendrixon		
Dec. 7, 1820	George Fraker—Nelly Brown		
Dec. 16, 1820	Isaac Stephens—Ann Humphreys		
Dec. 28, 1820	Henry Nichols—Patsy Watson		
Jan. 2, 1821	John Williams—Susannah Sehorn		
Jan. 3, 1821	James Martin—Margaret Long		
Jan. 4, 1821	Joseph Miller—Priscilla Hale		
Jan. 21, 1821	William Wattinberger—Elizabeth Kennedy		
Jan. 31, 1821	William Ruple—Nancy Allison	Isaac Hair	
Feb. 3, 1821	David Robinson—Nancy Jenkins	Clark Ellis	
Feb. 7, 1821	James C. Mansfield—Rebeccah G. Chester		
Feb. 10, 1821	Joseph B. Gilman—Sarah Gammon		
Feb. 16, 1821	John Isenberg—Hannah Pitcock	Daniel Isenberg	
Feb. 20, 1821	William Primmer—Mary Elliot		
Mar. 7, 1821	Robert Bean—Patsy Crouch		
Mar. 11. 1821	Stephen Brown—Betsy Tucker		
Mar. 13, 1821	John Moore—Sarah Nelson		
Mar. 14, 1821	Dan D. Andrew—Nancy Tyler		
Mar. 15, 1821	Richard Martain—Achah Hunt		
Mar. 15, 1821	John Andes—Polly Harvey		
Mar. 19, 1821	Wilson Scott—Mary Presser		
Mar. 22, 1821	Moses Ingersol—Cathrine Cebler		
April 1, 1821	William Barnet—Mary Edwards		
April 5, 1821	George Freeman—Sarah Watson		
April 28, 1821	John Peterson—Milly Carr		
May 1, 1821	David R. Shanks—Rebekah Hair		
May 5, 1821	Isaac Babb—Anna English		
May 16, 1821	James McLin—Jane Cunningham		
May 23, 1821	Willis Debord—Catherine Lilburn		
June 7, 1821	John Painter—Polly Newberry		
June 7, 1821	Charles Barnes—Betsy Edwards		
June 12, 1821	Abraham Britten—Nancy Brannon		
July 19, 1821	John Cloyd—Rebecca Patton		
July 20, 1821	David Hufman—Rachel Buth		
July 25, 1821	James Broyles—Sally Shoun		

Date	Male	Female	Bondman
July 28, 1821	Edward Davenport—Margaret Fawbush		
July 28, 1821	Ambrose Harrison—Harriet Miller	Thomas Williams	
July 31, 1821	Jeremiah Simpson—Elizabeth Lautermilt		
Aug. 5, 1821	Samuel Lewis—Elizabeth Pitcock	Samuel Douglass	
Aug. 7, 1821	Samuel G. Bayles—Fernanda Brown		
Aug. 16, 1821	William Broyles—Margaret Green		
Sept. 2, 1821	Joshua Swanger—Nancy Howard		
Sept. 4, 1821	Andrew Freeman—Nancy Jones		
Sept. 9, 1821	Daniel Crown—Elizabeth Bean		
Sept. 27, 1821	George Hinkle—Ann Zetty		
Oct. 2, 1821	Jacob Bacon—Elizabeth Kebler	George Jackson	
Oct. 9, 1821	Edward Malon—Margaret Castiel		
Oct. 21, 1821	Jacob Barnes—Ann Martin		
Oct. 25, 1821	Henry Jones—Aggey Francis		
Nov. 1, 1821	Robert Rustin—Margaret McGee		
Nov. 1, 1821	Jacob Jackson—Nancy Bacon		
Nov. 6, 1821	James H. Cochran—Jane Barkeley		
Nov. 22, 1821	Samuel S. Bell—Lem McCray		
Nov. 29, 1821	David Kitsmiller—Elizabeth Hughes		
Dec. 2, 1821	William Parker—Cinthia Gaines		
Dec. 4, 1821	Philip Babb—Artemesia Hale		
Dec. 6, 1821	John Melvin—Rachel Delaney		
Dec. 6, 1821	Daniel Delaney—Elizabeth McGhee		
Dec. 11, 1821	Simpson Charlton—Sarah Collins		
Dec. 25, 1821	Anthony Rankins—Margaret Gray		
Dec. 27, 1821	Isaac McPherson—Elizabeth Kinnedy		
Dec. 30, 1821	Nicholas Pring—Lucy Franklin		
Jan. 9, 1822	William Carson—Rachel Martin		
Jan. 10, 1822	John Nelson—Catherine Sliger		
Jan. 16, 1822	Joseph Mitchell—Margaret Boyd		
Jan. 18, 1822	Reuben Crouch—Polly Kincheloe		
Feb. 4, 1822	Martin Medlock—Nancy Mitchell		
Mar. 5, 1822	Thomas Pearce—Susannah Myers		
Mar. 14, 1822	Leonard Collier—Charlotte Slagle		
Mar. 25, 1822	Abraham Winkler—Elizabeth Stormer		
April 5, 1822	John Garin—Ruth Brummit		
April 10, 1822	Nathaniel Lunsford—Eliza Waldren		
May 6, 1822	Josiah Parker—Honer Gaines		
May 7, 1822	John Jones—Clarissa Sevier		
May 24, 1822	Thomas Pitcock—Elizabeth Carp		
June 1, 1822	Charles Quillen—Harriet Gyre		
June 19, 1822	Adam Sell—Margaret Miller		
July 8, 1822	John Bottles—Susan Patton		

Date	Male	Female	Bondman
July 22, 1822	Isaac Hair—Lavinah Susong		
July 25, 1822	Christopher Murray—Susan Depew		
Aug. 14, 1822	Robert Pore—Jane Ricker		
Aug. 19, 1822	James Acton—Zilla Bayles		
Aug. 22, 1822	James Whitson—Jemima Ramsey		
Aug. 27, 1822	Reese Browning—Hannah Boyd		
Aug. 29, 1822	Joseph Sherrill—Rachel Webb		
Sept. 4, 1822	Robert Aiken—Nancy Kennedy		
Sept. 5, 1822	Jacob Reser—Eliza Leakes		
Sept. 5, 1822	Valentine Brown—Catherine Edwards		
Sept. 5, 1822	James C. Davis—Rachel Tilson		
Sept. 12, 1822	Landford Crouch—Elizabeth Beam		
Sept. 12, 1822	Thomas Sliger—Mary Ann Kiker		
Sept. 16, 1822	John Walters—Margaret Kyker		
Sept. 19, 1822	Michael Clem—Nancy Hunt		
Sept. 22, 1822	John Britten—Catherine Hensley		
Sept. 24, 1822	Seth Waddell—Nancy McGhee		
Oct. 10, 1822	Adam Surbey—Mary McLien	Joseph Shields	
Oct. 14, 1822	George Little—Barbary Kelly		
Oct. 20, 1822	Joseph Million—Elizabeth Walters		
Oct. 26, 1822	John Eberly—Susannah Lineberger		
Oct. 29, 1822	Allen H. Matthews—Judith L. McConnel		
Nov. 12, 1822	William Feezle—Jerutia Pring		
Nov. 16, 1822	Simon Gresham—Sally Paste		
Nov. 16, 1822	John Hice—Ann Cassady	Robert Cassady	
Nov. 19, 1822	George Irvin—Judah Comby		
Nov. 20, 1822	Dillard Love—Margaret Young		
Nov. 21, 1822	Jacob Huffman—Peggy Mark		
Nov. 25, 1822	John Engle—Pheta Humphreys		
Nov. 25, 1822	Lesley Ford—Sarah Jackson		
Nov. 29, 1822	James Barnes—Margaret Grimley		
Dec. 3, 1822	John P. Chrisley—Rebecca G. Kumray		
Dec. 10, 1822	Jonathan Depew—Minerva Tipton		
Dec. 14, 1822	William Ford—Achsash Ford		
Dec. 14, 1822	James Lather—Sarah Masannis		
Dec. 22, 1822	Hosea Wrenshey—Mary McAdams		
Dec. 25, 1822	John Scott—Polly Clifford	John V. Bovill	
Dec. 25, 1822	George Brown—Mary Miller		
Dec. 26, 1822	John Brown—Nancy Clows		
Dec. 30, 1822	Gabriel Brown—Sarah Bayless		
Jan. 6, 1823	Alfred Duncan—Rhody Douglas		
Jan. 9, 1823	Joseph Burts—Elizabeth Young		
Jan. 17, 1823	Samuel Waddell—Violet Bayles	George Ekins	

Date	Male	Female	Bondman
Jan. 23, 1823	Samuel Lyle—Casandra Boring		
Jan. 27, 1823	Shederick Murray—Sally Hunt		Christopher Murray
Feb. 1, 1823	Charles Collins—Nancy Miller		William White
Feb. 12, 1823	Richard Dunlap—Mary Barnet		John Dunlap
Feb. 17, 1823	Ephriam McGloughlin—Elizabeth Barnes		
Feb. 19, 1823	John Hyder—Anne Worthington		
Feb. 25, 1823	William Seahorn—Ann Williams		John Williams
Feb. 26, 1823	Noding Hill—Ruth Brown		
Mar. 10, 1823	James Dosser—Jane Shoemaker		Ira Green
Mar. 11, 1823	John Tipton Boring—Elizabeth Threewit		
Mar. 14, 1823	John Harvey—Polly Engle		George Harvey
Mar. 20, 1823	Thomas Smith—Libby Tucker		David McGinnis
Mar. 22, 1823	John Hair—Aery Hail		Henry Hair
Mar. 23, 1823	Elijah Ellis—Jane McAdams		
Mar. 24, 1823	Leeroy Campbell—Ann Shields		
Mar. 30, 1823	John Wills—Carline Boren		William Snodgrass
April 2, 1823	Jesse McGinnis—Ann Reed		Mark T. Anderson
April 3, 1823	Reuben Anders—Rebecca Summers		Charles Basket
April 4, 1823	Moses Delashmet—Nancy Salts		John Jones
April 5, 1823	Samuel Holmes—Rachel Miller		Isaac McPherson
April 10, 1823	John Bedsauls—Polly Jones		Jesse Hendrickson
April 17, 1823	Claibourne Moore—Sally Morgan		William Dykes
April 26, 1823	Absolom Boring—Betsy Ruble		William White
April 28, 1823	Adam Garns—Elizabeth McAdams		
May 17, 1823	John Pofford—Sarah Ann Thompson		
May 19, 1823	James W. Wiley—Eliza Gillespie		
May 20, 1823	Solmon Vance, Jr.—Elizabeth Moor		
May 20, 1823	Daniel Barkley—Jane Shields		
May 22, 1823	Peter R. Miller—Sarah Deakins		
May 27, 1823	James Brown—Rachel George		E. F. Sevier
May 27, 1823	John F. Hannah—Grace Telford		
May 29, 1823	James Davison—Mary Ellis		John Crawford
June 7, 1823	David Carder—Susannah Morgan		Reuben Rogers
June 8, 1823	Asa Cook—Margaret Hammer		Henry King, Jr.
June 9, 1823	Jesse Tinker—Ally Norris		William S. Erwin
June 9, 1823	Richard Deakins—Isabella Beard		
June 19, 1823	Jacob Douglas—Polly Bacon		Samuel Douglas
June 19, 1823	Solomon Beals—Sally Stewart		
June 19, 1823	Robert Greene—Barsha Yeager		
June 27, 1823	Hugh P. Young—Esther Beard		
June 29, 1823	Thomas Lee—Nancy Hail		
July 20, 1823	Vincent Bull—Lydia Setseller		
July 31, 1823	William Hodges—Mary Ann Snyder		

Date	Male	Female	Bondman
July 31, 1823	Jeremiah Brown—Polly Starmer		
Aug. 1, 1823	Joseph Smith—Rachel M. Clark		
Aug. 12, 1823	Samuel Spurgen—Rosannah Duncan		
Aug. 17, 1823	Roland Hodges—Margaret Ellis		Jonathan Grass
Aug. 19, 1823	Rowland P. Murray—Ann Gallaway		
Aug. 19, 1823	Andrew Blythe—Debby Andrews		
Aug. 26, 1823	Stephen Pratt—Nancy Workman		
Aug. 27, 1823	Thomas McMackin—Ann Blair		William Crawford
Aug. 28, 1823	John Robinson—Ann Jones		Ezekiel Lyon
Sept. 6, 1823	Isaac Hammer—Catherine Bogart		George Hays
Sept. 7, 1823	Harvey Hamilton—Lydia Smith		Joseph Smith
Sept. 11, 1823	Ephraim Goins—Elizabeth Parker		
Sept. 23, 1823	Jacob Murr—Nancy Boyd		Rease Browning
Sept. 25, 1823	John Edwards—Sarah Hopkins		
Sept. 27, 1823	Michael Hoyle—Ann L. Mathes		
Oct. 14, 1823	Christopher Haines—Deanna Job		
Oct. 26, 1823	Johnson Edgemon—Rebecca Piercy		
Oct. 29, 1823	Duke Ruble—Sarah Slaughter		
Nov. 10, 1823	Barney Sanders—Mary Rigsby		
Nov. 13, 1823	William Snodgrass—Orpha Smith		
Nov. 21,1823	Austin Collins—Jemima McClure		
Nov. 21, 1823	Charles Ferrel—Mary Odle		
Nov. 24, 1823	Jonathan Prather—Rosanna Broyles		
Nov. 30, 1823	James Williams—Mary Tilson		
Dec. 14, 1823	Charles Bacon—Anny Hale		
Dec. 16, 1823	Frederick A. Rose—Theodocia Vance		
Jan. 1, 1824	William Smith—Mary Gyer		
Jan. 5, 1824	Jonothan Range—Fatha Kelley		
Jan. 10, 1824	Andrew E. Ball—Sarah Moore		
Jan. 11, 1824	Joseph Bean—Mary Sliger		
Jan. 20, 1824	George Fink—Sarah Gibson		
Jan. 22, 1824	Sylvester Ryland—May Hays		
Jan. 27, 1824	Jacob Phillips—Elizabeth White		
Feb. 3, 1824	Quillen Parker—Lucy Deen		
Feb. 9, 1824	Jesse Austin—Camilla Bean		
Feb. 12, 1824	David Sellers—Margaret Miars		
Feb. 15, 1824	John Oliver—Elizabeth Campbell		
Feb. 19, 1824	Jacob Harmon—Lucinda Gann		
Feb. 22, 1824	Hiram Swanay—Ruth Taylor		
Mar. 8, 1824	Anguish McDonald—Polly Moore		
Mar. 16, 1824	Lemuel Oliver—Polly Taylor		
Mar. 21, 1824	Tipton Boring—Ruth Howard		
April 1, 1824	William Patten—Melinda W. Jordan		

Date	Male	Female	Bondman
April 10, 1824	Henry Wolf—Nancy Kincheloe		
April 24, 1824	Adam Hope—Mary Carson		
May 6, 1824	Solomon Wittenbarger—Polly Humphreys		
May 10, 1824	John Nelson—Lucinda Lisenby		
May 12, 1824	John Stephens—Jane Scott	Wilson Scott	
May 23, 1824	Adam Slyger—Matilda Brown	William Bayles	
June ....., 1824	John J. McMackin—Isabel C. Blair		
June 7, 1824	Jacob Range—Anne Hammer	Jonathan Hammer	
June 15, 1824	George Pointer—Jane B. Temple	Jas. C. Simpson	
June 15, 1824	Jacob Boyd—Margaret Gervin	David Boyer	
July 1, 1824	Peter Emmet—Rachael Caruthers	Saml. Caruthers	
July 8, 1824	Samuel Brown—Elizabeth Boyer	J. W. Roberts	
July 12, 1824	Hiram Forbush—Nancy Milburn	Jas. Crouch	
July 15, 1824	Joseph Smith—Jane McCadell		
July 27, 1824	Abraham Smith—Elizabeth J. Stuart		
Aug. 8, 1824	John Kitzmiller—Louisa Devault		
Aug. 9, 1824	John McCurrey—Sarah Embree		
Aug. 19, 1824	David Clark—Jemima Jester	B. Bean	
Aug. 25, 1824	Nathaniel Haris—Hannah Ford		
Aug. 25, 1824	Samuel McKeehan—Susannah Overhots	Samuel Overholts	
Aug. 25, 1824	Daniel Zimmerman—Catharine Miller		
Aug. 31, 1824	Solomon Dinkin—Susan Parker		
Aug. 31, 1824	Isaiah Rose—Cassa Long	John Rose	
Sept. 2, 1824	Isaac Nelson—Martha Vauskoe	John Nelson	
Sept. 3, 1824	Benjamin Ford—Polly Ford	John Ford	
Sept. 9, 1824	Thomas Bible—Ann Eliza Wilson	John Ryland	
Sept. 9, 1824	Michael Wattenberger—Nancy Whistler	Jacob Whistler	
Sept. 16, 1824	William Mitchell—Mary Bucheighan	H. Swaney	
Sept. 23, 1824	Jacob Good—Elizabeth Ricard	Lewis Ricard	
Sept. 24, 1824	Charles Lisenberg—Susan Carr	D. Kinney	
Sept. 27, 1824	George Odneal—Nancy Reave	Levi Feaster	
Sept. 28, 1824	Mordicai Ford—Nancy Hyte	John Ford	
Oct. 5, 1824	David C. Hunter—Maria Stephenson		
Oct. 14, 1824	Samuel Bell—Nancy W. Mathes	E. S. Mathes	
Oct. 14, 1824	Joseph Bottles—Ann Lineberger		
Oct. 14, 1824	John Coppenger—Elizabeth Rodgers		
Oct. 16, 1824	John Houston—Elizabeth Kelley	Dungan Houston	
Oct. 18, 1824	Skelton Taylor—Mary McCray	Jacob Miller	
Oct. 21, 1824	Peter Wian—May Eva Overholt		
Oct. 30, 1824	Peter Slagle—Misse Brumit	John Slagle	
Nov. 4, 1824	Thomas Beard—Jane Hall		

Date	Male	Female	Bondman
Nov. 6, 1824	Robert Nelson—Louise Pratt		George Kirk
Nov. 17, 1824	John Rickard—Rebecca Mash		Elias Bowman
Nov. 18, 1824	William Hart—Orry Boren		J. A. Wilds
Nov. 24, 1824	John Walker—Creasy Martin		James Squibb
Nov. 25, 1824	William Ellison—Sarah Williams		William A. Seehorn
Nov. 30, 1824	John Deakins—Jane Russell		James Deakins
Dec. 1, 1824	John E. Casson—Mary E. Harris		
Dec. 4, 1824	Richard Chinouth—Patsy Ellis		Joseph Chinouth
Dec. 4, 1824	Thomas Linder—Ann Oliver		Peter Ruble
Dec. 11, 1824	John Little—Ruth Boren		William Wheeler
Dec. 13, 1824	Samuel Robinson—Martha Chester		James Robinson
Dec 14, 1824	Abner Beals—Winny Owens		John Tucker
Dec. 16, 1824	Robert Russell—Elener Terry		James Guynon
Dec. 17, 1824	Thomas Hampton—Joanna Renno		Sm'l. Headrick
Dec. 17, 1824	Elijah E. Smith—Catharine Brown		
			Abraham Brown
Dec. 18, 1824	Richard Basket—Lucy McNabb		Samuel Chapman
Dec. 21, 1824	Thomas Stanberry—Sarah Cass		William P. Chester
Dec. 23, 1824	James Leslie—Sarah Campbell		Jon Leslie
Dec. 24, 1824	Peechy Harrison—Jane Clark		A. Finch
Dec. 27, 1824	Adam Shipley—Catherine Brown		Benjamin Shipley
Dec. 30, 1824	George Speers—Cynthia Fulkes		Leven Speers
Dec. 30, 1824	John Kennedy—Cynthia Bakeley		
Jan. 2, 1825	Thomas Carroll—Ann Maiden		Samuel Maiden
Jan. 4, 1825	Moses Thompson—Elizabeth Smith		George Smith
Jan. 6, 1825	Daniel Devault—Mary Miller		Nicholas Devault
Jan. 6, 1825	James Payne—Sarah Smith		D. Kenney
Jan. 11, 1825	Andrew Miller—Nancy Miller		Simon Miller
Jan. 23, 1825	Jonah Lilburn—Mary Hertsell		
Jan. 25, 1825	Caleb Cox—Ann Carriger		John Cox
Jan. 29, 1825	David Jenkins—Nancy Boren		
Jan. 29, 1825	Isaac Bowman—Agnes Young		
Jan. 31, 1825	Christian Grove—Jane Lacky		
Feb. 3, 1825	Aaron Kees—Hannah Nelson		John Nelson
Feb. 12, 1825	Isaac Fulkerson—Catherine Bacon		Charles Bacon
Feb. 15, 1825	Green K. Cessna—Maria L. Vance		
Feb. 17, 1825	Stephen Bailes—Nancy Milburn		Achilles Pratt
Feb. 21, 1825	Hiram Swaney—Ruth Taylor		
Feb. 24, 1825	Henry Kitzmiller—Elizabeth Carr		
Mar. 3, 1825	John Goforth—Nancy Chandler		Jonah Lilburn
Mar. 5, 1825	Sterling Moore—Elizabeth Holland		Wm. Gillespie
Mar. 8, 1825	Isaac Jaques—Peggy Grimsly		David Gibson
Mar. 9, 1825	Benjamin Hinkle—Lucinda Terry		Jas. Maydwell

Date	Male	Female	Bondman
Mar. 10, 1825	Joseph Willit—Susan Stout		John W. Simpson
Mar. 10, 1825	James Houston—Sarah Caruthers		John Houston
Mar. 12, 1825	Joseph Porter—Nancy Daniels		
Mar. 14, 1825	John E. Peterson—Winny Webb		John Rose
Mar. 15, 1825	John Hains—Eliza Cobinger		
Mar. 21, 1825	Jacob Zimmerman—Sarah Bowman		
Mar. 22, 1825	Charles Harrison—Elizabeth Kellor		
			William Harrison
Mar. 29, 1825	Thomas Russell—Caroline Smith		Jas H. Jones
April 1,1825	Samuel Kennedy—Martha Massengale		
April 2, 1825	Elbert Freeman—Margaret Smawley		
			Robert H. Hale
April 2, 1825	Jeremiah Hale—Nancy Hunt		E. W. Bacon
April 4, 1825	William Haws—Melinda Kibler		
April 12, 1825	Thomas Bell—Elizabeth Ferguson		John Duncan
April 12, 1825	Reuben Tompkins—Ceneth Lisenby		Wm. S. Erwin
April 12, 1825	Elijah Shipley—Nancy Hunt		Enoch Shipley
April 19, 1825	Thomas King—Elizabeth Rose		George A. King
April 30, 1825	Isaac Keizer—Mary Bradley		Jonathan Bradley
May 6, 1825	Henry Young—Catherine Miller		
May 7, 1825	Samuel Pointer—Hannah Johnston		
May 10, 1825	John Gibson—Rhoda Barnes		Josiah Wood
May 19, 1825	Ancil Lane—Sidney Woods		Benjamin Cary
May 25, 1825	Isaac Headrick—Elizabeth Copass		Joshua Boren
May 26,1825	James Billingsley—Sarah Hale		E. W. Bacon
May 26, 1825	James Crouch—Susannah Bowman		A. Martin
May 29, 1825	Jesse Mathes—Nancy Brown		Abraham Brown
May 30, 1825	James Bradley—Levina Buck		Henry Saylor
June 7, 1825	Alexander Anderson—Eliza Rose Deadrick		
June 27, 1825	Samuel Williams—Rebeca Morison		
July 14, 1825	Absolum W. Rush—Polly Morrison		Daniel Yeager
July 19, 1825	Jeremiah Murr—Rachel Click		Joseph Bale
July 31, 1825	Henry E. Ruble—Phoebe Hunter		Nat Kelsey
Aug. 4, 1825	Duston G. Murrill—Elizabeth Emmerson		
Aug. 17, 1825	Allen Fulkerson—Ruth Gott		Wm. Jackson
Aug. 20, 1825	Jeremiah Dean—Susan Parks		
Aug. 21, 1825	James Deakens—Anna Walker		
Aug. 22, 1825	James Hodges—Mary Kitzmiller		John Alison
Aug. 25, 1825	Joseph Walker—Jane Chandler		
Aug. 30, 1825	Robert Glenn—Noney Patton		
Sept. 2, 1825	William Moon—Mahala Scalph		Mark Anderson
Sept 8, 1825	Jonathan Bacon—Debby Bains		
Sept. 8, 1825	John Hale—Elizabeth Smith		William Ellis

Date	Male	Female	Bondman
Sept. 13, 1825	Jacob Laudermilk—Dorcas Boren		Wm. Wheeler
Sept. 17, 1825	Seth Smith—Elizabeth Miller		Eliss Boman
Sept. 21, 1825	Matheas Broyles—Ann Bayles		
Sept. 29, 1825	Edward Million—Ann Bayless		
Oct. 1, 1825	James Owens—Sarah Jones		Greenbury Delishmut
Oct. 1, 1825	Jesse Payne, Sr.—Mahaley McCoy		John Squibb
Oct. 6, 1825	John McNees—Maryane Greenway		M. T. Anderson
Oct. 6, 1825	Kinchen Kelly—Isabella Young		Henry Miller
Oct. 12, 1825	Samuel E. Edwards—Elizabeth Jobe		
Oct. 13, 1825	John Berkley—Mary Grayham		John Bartley
Oct. 13, 1825	Joshua Bowers—Anne Murry		Levi Bowers
Oct. 25, 1825	Wilson Taylor—Sally Felts		Jacob Taylor
Oct. 29, 1825	James Brearly—Elizabeth Click		
Nov. 1, 1825	Samuel Beard—Catherine Bricker		Joseph L. Hale
Nov. 4, 1825	William Fletcher—Maria Robinson		Joseph Bean
Nov. 5, 1825	Daniel P. Bayles—Lidia Flaer		
Nov. 8, 1825	James Mitchell—Elizabeth Bacon		
Nov. 12, 1825	Henry Boyd—Sarah Barly		David Boyd
Nov. 17, 1825	Loid Ford—Matilda Jackson		Grant Ford
Nov. 28, 1825	John Creamer—Margaret McNeal		
Dec. 2, 1825	Samuel Martin—Nancy Shields		James Reed
Dec. 8, 1825	George G. Jackson—Nancy Campbell		Moses Osborn
Dec. 15, 1825	Thomas Bacon—Sally Barren		
Dec. 27, 1825	William Shields—Polly Mathews		Henry McCracken
Dec. 29, 1825	John Cronwell—Mary Wheelock		John Kincheloe
Dec. 31, 1825	Jesse Harrison—Geriah Medlock		
No. Date	Daniel Barkley—Jane Shields		
No Date	Samuel Stanbury—Matilda McCollam		
Jan. 2, 1826	Elan Johnson—Martha Young C. Parker		
Jan. 3, 1826	David Holt—Isabella Templin		
Jan. 15, 1826	Jonathan Corder—Sarah White		David White
Feb. 6, 1826	Thomas Watson—Harriet Job		
Feb. 7, 1826	James Russell—Rachel Allison		
Feb. 7, 1826	Abraham Saylor—Abigal Melvin		Henry Saylor
Feb. 8, 1826	William Ellis—Mary McAdam		S. Crawford
Feb. 9, 1826	John Stout—Rachel Irvine		Joseph Crouch
Feb. 9, 1826	Elijah Wilson—George Brown		
Feb. 16, 1826	Frances Clark—Delitha Seaball		Isaac Williams
Feb. 18, 1826	Horatio Morrison—Ruth Ford		
Mar. 13, 1826	Vincent Boring—Loisa Little		
Mar. 14, 1826	Joseph Stuart—Elizabeth Miller		Alexander Stuart
Mar. 15, 1826	William Denton—Rachel Gibson		Josiah Wood
Mar. 23, 1826	Shadrack Nelson—Ibby Whitson		

Date	Male	Female	Bondman
April 3, 1826	Abraham Miller—Nancy Hale		James R. Simpson
April 6, 1826	James Simpson—Mary Ann Murray		Aaron Finch
April 16, 1826	James Cooper—Nancy Parker		Elan Johnston
April 20, 1826	Joseph Brown—Nancy Edwards		Cowell Brown
May 4, 1826	Peter Dotson—Margaret Stansbury		Wm. P. Chester
May 4, 1826	James Nelson—Elinor Parker		William Nelson
May 11, 1826	Robert Gray—Agnes Chinnoth		Joseph Chinoth
May 11, 1826	Jacob Long—Mary Riddle		John Nelson
May 15, 1826	John Carroll—Elizabeth Coppick		Luke Carroll
May 25, 1826	Jeremiah Hale—Mary Crouch		Joseph Crouch
May 27, 1826	Thomas Coldwell—Cloe Wheelock		James Whillock
June 3, 1826	James Tilson—Eunis Tilson		Gabriel McInturff
June 22, 1826	Enos Campbell—Jane Cloyd		
June 29, 1826	Hellings D. Tilson—Peggy Ann Murray		Wm. S. Ervin
July 6, 1826	Jeremiah Keys—Mary Forguson		John Nelson
July 8, 1826	Edward Hammon—Nancy Cade		Duke Rubel
July 10, 1826	Benjamin Tompkins—Nancy Brown		
July 15, 1826	Michael Crouse—Rebecca Young		Hugh P. Young
July 20, 1826	John Nelson—Easter Forguson		Aaron Keys
July 20, 1826	William Brizely—Sabra Britner		Chas. Grimes
July 25, 1826	Gilbert F. Patterson—Margaret Bayles		Isaac Haire
July 26, 1826	Hagan Nine—Elizabeth Randolph		
July 28, 1826	Thomas Dunham—Nancy Flemming		Jonathan Bacon
Aug. 10, 1826	John Duncan—Rachel F. Duncan		Josiah Conly
Aug. 15, 1826	Andrew Odell—Nancy Kelsy		J. D. Givin
Aug. 16, 1826	James Quimby—Elizabeth Chany		Charles Basket
Aug. 21, 1826	Henry Ingle—Amanda Graham		George McNees
Aug. 24, 1826	Charles Lineberger—Ann Lopwasser		
Sept. 12, 1826	Henry W. Collins—Margaret Fisher		E. Barkley
Sept. 14, 1826	Lewis Fondwell—Ruth Ann Smith		W. Atkinson
Sept. 16, 1826	Jonas L. King—Mary Barnes		Henry King
Sept. 21, 1826	Elijah Bacon—Martha Squibb		
Sept. 28, 1826	Joshua Leonard—Rhoda Sweet		Jacob Brown, Jr.
Sept. 29, 1826	William Mowdy—Nancy Warren		
Oct. 5, 1826	John Gray—Melinda Coff		
Oct. 12, 1826	Samuel Bayles—Nancy Mitchel		John Martin
Oct. 14, 1826	Alexander Adams—Lindy Brown		Ancil Lane
Oct. 19, 1826	Jacob Clouse—Sarah Tilson		W. A. Irwin
Oct. 24, 1826	Thomas Mercer—Henrietta Duke		John Green
Oct. 26, 1826	Emanuel Good—Elizabeth Copp		Benjamin Copp
Oct. 30, 1826	William H. Young—Emilin Jikes Tipton		
Nov. 1, 1826	William Nicholas—Ann Overholer		

Date	Male	Female	Bondman
Nov. 1, 1826	Samuel Slyger—Mary Brown		
Nov. 2, 1826	Lawrence Leonard—Mary Guyne		
Nov. 14, 1826	William A. Harris—Elizabeth Cariger		
Nov. 16, 1826	Samuel D. Bayles—Basmath Peoples		
Nov. 19, 1826	Joseph Hinkle—Barbara Croompeckas		
Nov. 23, 1826	Benjamin P. Hopkins—Ruth Tinker		
Nov. 29, 1826	Richard Baskett—Rachel Hartman	Payne Squibb	
Dec. 2, 1826	Jonah Mahoney—Synthia Irwin	Chandler Irwin	
Dec. 3, 1826	Abel March—Anny Martin	Henry March	
Dec. 6, 1826	David Brown—Polly Campbell		
Dec. 16, 1826	John Smith—Ruth Boren	David Stuart	
Dec. 21, 1826	Daniel Swords—Polly Newman		
Dec. 23, 1826	Michael Shanks—Hannah Cairy		
Dec. 26, 1826	John Rigesly—Maria Ellis	Joseph Beals	
Dec. 30, 1826	Nathan Shipley, Jr.—Hannah Miller		
Jan. 5, 1827	Elkanah Keener—Elizabeth Lamon	John Booth	
Jan. 12, 1827	Aron Coppeck—Olive Carrol	Luke Carrol	
Jan. 12, 1827	William C. Collor—Elizabeth Barnes		
Jan. 13, 1827	Hamilton Copeland—Margaret Irwin	Jno. L. Irwin	
Jan. 15, 1827	John Smith—Mary Hoss	Isaac Williams	
Jan. 18, 1827	William Looney—Betsy West		
Jan. 19, 1827	William Kelsey—Evelina Astin		
Jan. 27, 1827	Hardin Norris—Elizabeth Whitson	James Norris	
Feb. 1, 1827	John Kirk—Margaret Kelsely	George Kirk	
Feb. 3, 1827	William Nelson—Sarah Owen		
Feb. 6, 1827	Richard Suttles—Harriet Aleger	Ellis Suttles	
Feb. 15, 1827	Robert Treadway—Artimacy Bayles	D. O. Donnel	
Feb. 19, 1827	John McCracken—Hannah Tucker		
Feb. 28, 1827	William Mathes—Eleanor McLin	Andrew Odell	
Mar. 3, 1827	Daniel Weatherford—Nancy Briant	Jacob Brom	
Mar. 7, 1827	James Reed—Mary McCoy		
Mar. 8, 1827	James Moore—Mahaley Scalf	George King	
Mar. 8, 1827	John Davison—Lydia Leslie	Luke Rubel	
Mar. 10, 1827	John Garland—Camilla Bean	John Lackey	
Mar. 16, 1827	John Barkley—Elizabeth Charleton		
Mar. 20, 1827	Thomas W. Hunt—Mary Young		
Mar. 21, 1827	Henry Massingale—Lavina Hoss		
Mar. 20, 1827	Jacob Cheats—Sarah Chinuth		
Mar. 22, 1827	John Van—Nancy Matlock		
Mar. 24, 1827	James Miller—Elizabeth Devault	Richard Cave	
Mar. 27, 1827	Jacob Sheets—Sarah Chinouth	James Fitzgerald	
April 2, 1827	Lewis Rankin—Mary Gray	Edward West, Jr.	
April 6, 1827	Charles Cox—Rebeca Elsey		

Date	Male	Female	Bondman
April 7, 1827	Payne Squibb—Dicy Hunt		John Squibb
April 11, 1827	James Robison—Ascaia Jenkins		David Robison
April 12, 1827	John Matlock—Malinda Ellis		Henry Fox
April 27, 1827	David Birdwell—Malinda Brown		H. D. Greer
April 28, 1827	Vincent Tapp—Rachel Burris		Wm. S. Erwin
May 5, 1827	Aaron Pitcock—Blanche Walden		Thomas Pitcock
May 7, 1827	John Salts—Susan Pring		
May 15, 1827	Elijah Shannon—Eliza Simpson		J. Howard
May 18, 1827	John H. Thomas—Margaret Kelley		Fred Finslur
May 27, 1827	Elijah Fenchum—Theodocia Sargant		
May 27, 1827	Benjamin Hunt—Margaret Walker		Wm. B. Strain
May 31, 1827	Joshua Babb—Serrafina Smith		Lewis Anderson
June 2, 1827	George Jenkins—Polly Hodges		Wm. C. Nelson
June 13, 1827	Solomon Smith—Eliza Colson		
June 19, 1827	John Brown—Elizabeth Parker		
June 23, 1827	Richard Hail—Ibby Hill		George Jenkins
June 24, 1827	Jeremiah Million—Tempe Salts		
June 25, 1827	William Penhum—Susan Baker		
Aug. 2, 1827	Shedrick Murray, Jr.—Sarah Ferguson		Elijah Bacon
Aug. 6, 1827	James Kebler—Sarah Haws		
Aug. 21, 1827	Nathaniel McStuart—Sarah Mitchell		Thomas Purce
Aug. 27, 1827	John Brown—Polly Barry		Broxton Brown
Sept. 6, 1827	William Combs—Nancy Conkin		
Sept. 6, 1827	Alfred M. Marsh—Kuzen Lacky		
Sept. 11, 1827	Samuel Drake—Eliza Murry		Sam'l. W. Williams
Sept. 11, 1827	Robert Johnston—Letty Crocksell		Isaac Hartsell
Sept. 15, 1827	Robert Taylor—Anny Freeman		J. P. Taylor
Sept. 17, 1827	John Tipton—Salena Headrick		Sam'l. Headrick
Sept. 21, 1827	William Duncan—Elizabeth Bayles		
Sept. 20, 1827	Martin Carey—Anny Sherfey		
Sept. 30, 1827	Daniel Galloway—Hannah Gifford		Rowland Murray
Sept. 25, 1827	Isaac Newman—Nancy Hunt		Isaac Elser
Oct. 1, 1827	Christian Stover—Margaret Wolf		
Oct. 4, 1827	George Kennedy—Nancy Tedlock		John Purcell
Oct. 5, 1827	John Broyles—Elijah Bayles		
Oct. 4, 1827	Archibald Hail—Ann Gresham		
Oct. 9, 1827	Joseph Hilton—Catharine Robinson		
Oct. 17, 1827	Abraham E. Miller—Elizabeth Bacon		
Oct. 27, 1827	John Lowry Bedsalls—Mary Bacon		
Nov. 15, 1827	Samuel Criselus—Lucinda Kiker		L. Leonard
Nov. 17, 1827	Joseph Sheets—Rhody Grills		James Hale
Nov. 30, 1827	John Smith—Sarah Ann Fawbush		
Dec. 4, 1827	John Archer—Rebecca Smith		

Date	Male	Female	Bondman
Dec. 5, 1827	Jacob Linebarger—Mary Barnes		Joseph Bottles
Dec. 13, 1827	Jacob Broyles—Lucinda Broyles		
Dec. 20, 1827	John Graham—Mary Bayles		
Dec. 24, 1827	Samuel Kelsey—Mary McCleary		
Dec. 24, 1827	E. Odum—Mary Walker		
Dec. 25, 1827	William Irwin—Catherine Wheelock		
Dec. 26, 1827	Dominick February—Sarah Williams		
Jan. 5, 1828	Thomas Pitcock—Rebecca Bails		Aaron Pitcock
Jan. 6, 1828	Abraham Hicks—Elizabeth Sheppard		
Jan. 22, 1828	John Irwin—Alsey Bails		Joseph Beals
Jan. 24, 1828	James Boyd—Sarah Patterson		
Jan. 29, 1828	Elijah Embree—Mariah King		
Feb. 2, 1828	John Bayley—Delilah Broyles		Aaron Panter
Feb. 13, 1828	James Coggburn—Jane Mercer		
Feb. 20, 1828	John Stevens—Margaret Jarrett		Nicholas Payne
Feb. 26, 1828	James Reed—Mary McCoy		Geo. M. Odeneal
Mar. 2, 1828	Doctor William Mitchell—Elizabeth Carter		
Mar. 3, 1828	Daniel Weatherford—Nancy Briant		
Mar. 4, 1828	Samuel H. Stephens—Elizabeth Pierce		
Mar. 4, 1828	William Seebolt—Elizabeth Baker		
Mar. 6, 1828	Isaac Beals—Anny Pitcock		Solomon Beals
Mar. 26, 1828	Enoch Whitson—Elizabeth White		
Mar. 27, 1828	Jesse Brown—Betsy Wattenberger		
Mar. 27, 1828	Peter Hunt—Lethy Bayles		
April 4, 1828	Joseph Tilson—Mary White		William Tilson
April 11, 1828	George W. Nelson—Mary Harvey		
May 8, 1828	Thomas Mitchell—Sarah White		William Mitchell
May 31, 1828	Joseph Bowman—Aley Carr		Daniel Bowman
June 18, 1828	William McRoberts—Isabella Hunter		
June 30, 1828	Charles Slagle—Senah Meadow Wiatt		
July 8, 1828	Hiram Wilson—Mary Smith		
July 10, 1828	Thoma I. Harris—Catherine Keplinger		Wm. Dosser
July 10, 1828	J. Heter Crouch—Jemima McGuise		
July 24, 1828	Thomas Jackson—Delilah Heartsell		Samuel Henley
Aug. 8, 1828	Robert Hodge—Elizabeth Isenbergh		Joshua Gray
Aug. 12, 1828	Hennenan Henley—Flora Ann Snapp		
Aug. 12, 1828	Lausen Campbell—Mary McGhee		
Aug. 24, 1828	Thomas Ford—Elizabeth Chandley		Lloyd Ford
Aug. 26, 1828	Jesse Owens—Nancy Jones		
Aug. 28, 1828	Andrew Jones—Susannah Baker		James Small
Sept. 2, 1828	Peter Brown—Margaret H. Collett		
Sept. 2, 1828	Norris Williams—Margaret Needham		
Sept. 4, 1828	Samuel A. Stephens—Elizabeth Pierce		Josiah Conley

Date	Male	Female	Bondman
Sept. 8, 1828	Thomas Nelson—Eliza Tucker		
Sept. 10, 1828	George Belcher—Eliza Norton		
Sept. 11, 1828	Michael P. Light—Rhoda Ellis		Jas. P. Hulse
Sept. 17, 1828	John H. Snapp—Maria Kepple		W. P. Chester
Sept. 18, 1828	Allen Jones—Nancy Carson		Enoch Kincheloe
Sept. 24, 1828	Jacob Keplinger—Sarah E. Ruble		
Sept. 28, 1828	Owen Williams—Elizabeth Slagle		Henry Slagle
Sept. 30, 1828	John H. Warren—Margaret Good		David Stewart
Oct. 2, 1823	Thomas Watson—Marian Royston		
Oct. 8, 1828	Nathan Nelson—Elizabeth Mitchell		
Oct. 9, 1828	Daniel Stormer—Elizabeth Patterson		
			John McCorkle
Oct. 12, 1828	Silas Brown—Phebe Ann Andes		James Jones
Oct. 17, 1828	Jacob Kyker—Eliza Greer		Philip Balone
Oct. 25, 1828	William Vaughn—Edy Medlock		Smith Hunt
Oct. 26, 1828	Solomon Cellers—Polly Kelly		
Oct. 28, 1828	George Profet—Margaret Wheelock		Geo. W. Brown
Oct. 29, 1828	Israel McInturff—Elizabeth Webb		Gabriel McInturff
Oct. 30, 1828	John McNeal—Margaret Harmon		
Oct. 30, 1828	James Campbell—Ann White		
Nov. 4, 1828	John Jobe—Sarah Elsey		
Nov. 5, 1828	Isaac Miller—Elizabeth Ann Crumparker		
Nov. 6, 1828	Thomas McAdams—Elizabeth McNeale		
Nov. 18, 1828	William Campbell—Sarah Recard		Jno. B. Waddill
Nov. 20, 1828	John Reeser—Margaret Grien		Aaron Painter
Dec. 2, 1828	Rufus Scroggs—Maria Miller		
Dec. 7, 1828	Barnett Baxter—Melissa Cunningham		
Dec. 9, 1828	William Brazelton—Martha A. Gillespie		
Dec. 9, 1828	Benjamin Hussy—Jane Furgeson		
Dec. 9, 1828	James Morgan—Polly Ann Riddle		
Dec. 10, 1828	Ephriam Nelson—Elizabeth Capp		
Dec. 10, 1828	Benjamin Rodgers—Artemasia Rodgers		
Dec. 12, 1828	John G. Ruble—Esther Fine		
Dec. 23, 1828	James Biddle—Elizabeth Whister		
Jan. 1, 1829	Sam'l Hufman—Rebeckah Byerly		
Jan. 6, 1829	Jacob Snapp—Hepsabe Waddle		
Jan. 12, 1829	William Edwards—Eliza Brown		
Jan. 12, 1829	Jesse I. James—Mary Anna McGuire		
Jan. 14, 1829	George Farnsworth—Elizabeth Bartley		
Jan. 15, 1829	John Longmire—Elizabeth Range		Wm. S. Irwin
Jan. 22, 1829	John Harrison—Delilah McDaniel		Ambrose Harrison
Jan. 30, 1829	John Barron— Wright		Jonathan Bacon
Feb. 11, 1829	Othneal Bowman—Elizabeth Watson		

Date	Male	Female	Bondman
Feb. 15, 1829	Abram Miller—Barbary Sherfy		S. G. Sherfy
Mar. 1, 1829	Robert Britt—Nancy Nelson		Shadrack Nelson
Mar. 5, 1829	William Kincheloe—Minerva Hale		
Mar. 26, 1829	George Hickman—Nancy Ferguson		
Mar. 28, 1829	John McCall—Elizabeth Kennedy		
April 14, 1829	Daniel France—Martha Gervin		
April 16, 1829	Thomas Oliver—Margaret Mitchell		
April 27, 1829	Dannes Houston—Rebecca Pharez (Farris)		
April 28, 1829	Jonathan Ambrose—Mary Tinker—Gabriel McInturff		
May 7, 1829	William Bovell—Hester M. Doak		
May 25, 1829	Robert Johnston—Elizabeth Suttles		
June 3, 1829	John Collet—Mary Britten		Abraham Tucker
June 13, 1829	Solomon Smith—Eliza Colson		John Miller
June 16, 1829	Jesse Headrick—Edy Faubush		William Vaughn
June 24, 1829	Samuel Hofman—Ruth Smith		Daniel Kinney
June 25, 1829	Adam W. Garner or Ganns—Sophia Giger		
			D. C. Hunter
June 25, 1829	John N. Doak—Martha Snapp		
July 2, 1829	James Stuart—Mary M. Sevier		
July 15, 1829	John Houston—Mary Rose		Thomas King
July 28, 1829	James Moore—Sarah Mitchell		
July 28, 1829	Nathaniel Hale—Jane Melvin		John A. Wilds
Aug. 4, 1829	Josiah Conley—Mary Ann Allison		David Ferguson
Aug. 6, 1829	Solomon Sherfy—Acsean Deakins		James Deakins
Aug. 11, 1829	Samuel Bowman—Anne Crouch		Sam'l Anderson
Aug. 13, 1829	Charles Neal—Margaret Kennedy		George Hays
Aug. 18, 1829	Hugh Vance—Rachel Blair		Thos. Thompson
Aug. 21, 1829	Allen Tittle—Anney Clouse		Jeremiah Bogart
Sept. 1, 1829	Zaddock Lewis—Anne Marie Smith		Wm. Dosser
Sept. 7, 1829	Samuel Shannon—Elizabeth White		
Sept. 12, 1829	Lewis Scalf—Nancy Koziah		
Sept. 17, 1829	Henry Young—Deborah Hammer		
Sept. 19, 1829	Eleazer Payne—Elizabeth Looney		William Payne
Sept. 22, 1829	Aaron Brown—Mary Collet		John Smith
Sept. 29, 1829	Henry Sliger—Catherine Keplinger		Sm'l. Keplinger
Sept. 30, 1829	Ephriam Bird—Ellianor Mauk		
Oct. 3, 1829	John Blakley—Barbara Hays		John Pursell
Oct. 8, 1829	Chinouth Hale—Nancy Chase		Henry Chinouth
Oct. 12, 1829	Samuel Moore—Sarah Metcalf		Wm. S. Erwin
Oct. 25, 1829	Beverly Stanton—Mary Bayly		Ebeneza L. Patton
Oct. 27, 1829	Elkanah H. Howard—Mary Denton		
Oct. 28, 1829	John Dillingham—Mary Stephens		James Mears
Oct. 29, 1829	Joseph Jenkins—Ailey Keys		Robert Dyer

Date	Male	Female	Bondman
Oct. 30, 1829	William Bayles—Eliza Collins		Henry Gyer
Nov. 4, 1829	Jacob Hufhines—Anne Poore		Sam'l G. Chester
Nov. 24, 1829	John Ferjer—Teaney Slyger		John Slyger
Dec. 2, 1829	Abraham Snapp—Matilda Windell		
Dec. 3, 1829	William Cummins—Mary Nelson		
Dec. 3, 1829	Adam Sliger—Elizabeth Spradlin		Jonathan Bacon
Dec. 3, 1829	David Honeycut—Mary White		John White
Dec. 9, 1829	Thomas Nave—Louise Humphreys		
Dec. 12, 1829	David Wilson—Anne Glaze		George Brown
Dec. 13, 1829	Alexander Hurvey—Eliza Shanklin		John W. Hurvey
Dec 15, 1829	Absolom Deakins—Nancy McCray		Henry Deakins
Dec. 19, 1829	Solomon Fox—Eliza Whurley		Daniel Fox
Dec. 19, 1829	William Walters—Nancy Kiplinger		
Dec. 22, 1829	Joshua Jennings—Eliza Nelson		
Jan. 1, 1830	Ancil Lane—Elizabeth Cash		John White
Jan. 5, 1830	William Rains—Nancy Melvin		
Jan. 11, 1830	James White—Anne Humphries		
Jan. 14, 1830	Jacob Sherfey—Catherine Starr		Samuel Sherfey
Jan. 14, 1830	John Carithers—Polly Melvin		
Jan. 15, 1830	Joseph Hartman—Maria Pursell		Andrew Givin
Jan. 16, 1830	Laban Jackson—Nancy Elsey		Geo. Barron
Jan. 17, 1830	Thomas Day—Matilda Henley		
Jan. 17, 1830	Holden Shanks—Eliza Taylor		David Shanks
Jan. 22, 1830	David W. Patten—Annie L. Mathes		
Jan. 28, 1830	Daniel Fox—Anne Porter		Jno. Isombother
Feb. 3, 1830	John Sliger—Hester Brown		Jesse Brown
Feb. 5, 1830	Trenton Leach—Margaret Hufman		
Feb. 11, 1830	James L. Patrick—Margaret Ralston		
Feb. 18, 1830	William R. Dinwiddie—Martha Blakley		Jas. Blakley
Feb. 24, 1830	Joel Cooper—Sarah Boren		
Feb. 25, 1830	George Wilson—Elizabeth Messemore		
Mar. 2, 1830	Samuel Pugh—Sarah Gray		James H. Jones
Mar. 28, 1830	Andrew Coleman—Mary Needy		Jonah Marsh
Mar. 16, 1830	Jonathan Buck—Eliza Houston		Jonathan Kilby
Mar. 17, 1830	Robert A. Duncan—Jane Robertson		John Thompson
Mar. 23, 1830	Alexander Oliver—Nancy Duncome		Adam Casedy
Mar. 23, 1830	David C. Hunter—Achsah McCray		
Mar. 25, 1830	George Brown—Elizabeth Sands		Nathaniel Sands
Mar. 31, 1830	James Hale—Almira Bacon		
April 1, 1830	Isaac Starnes—Elizabeth Seebolt		John Coppinger
April 7, 1830	Peter Salts—Jane Bedsol		Hezekiah Bayles
April 10, 1830	Horatio Moss—Elizabeth Holts		John White
April 12, 1830	Hezekiah Brown—Ann Basket		Andrew Given

Date	Male	Female	Bondman
April 22, 1830	William Duncan—Elizabeth Buckingham		
			Jacob Taylor
April 27, 1830	James H. Gillespie—Sarahann Young		
May 5, 1830	Andrew McCoy—Polly Salts		Henry Boolman
May 6, 1830	Jacob Stanberry—Sarah Overholser		
May 26, 1830	Martin Kortz—Sarah Hunter		Washington Willett
May 20, 1830	Richard M. Linn—Rachel Blackmoore		
May 29, 1830	Daniel Bails—Rebeccah Andrews		
June 6, 1830	Elkanah McBroom—Roseannah Salts		
June 10, 1830	Charles Hartsell—Amanda Click		John Bedsell
June 22, 1830	Samuel Odell—Nancy Simpson		
June 29, 1830	Christian Slyger—Elizabeth Brown		William Hoss
June 29, 1830	Jonathan G. Haines—Sarah Williams		
June 30, 1830	Henry Kellow—Eliza Snapp		George W. Coffman
July 1, 1830	Richard Morris—Rhoda Hodges		Ellis H. Duncan
July 26, 1830	John A. Bowman—Mariah Worthington		Levi Bowers
Aug. 1, 1830	John Young—Jane W. Maxwell		
Aug. 11, 1830	Anthony Hartsell—Elizabeth Longmire		Robert Bean
Aug. 21, 1830	John R. Hunt—Margaret Holt		Joshua Williams
Sept. 4, 1830	William B. Strain—Martha Alice Stephenson		
Sept. 5, 1830	William Mayfield—Elizabeth Wright		
Sept. 9, 1830	Loyd A. Cox—Sarah English		
Oct. 1, 1830	James Russell—Mary W. Irwin		Wm. B. Strain
Oct. 1, 1830	Daniel Good—Sarah Cops		Lawrence Snapp
Oct. 11, 1830	Daniel Hufhines—Achsah Delaney		Robert Bean
Oct. 12, 1830	Jacob Keebler—Elizabeth McClain		Thos. Fulkerson
Oct. 18, 1830	Willoby Harvey—Margaret Parker		Hiram W. Clark
Oct. 18, 1830	Joseph Hunter—Margaret Miranda Harris		
Oct. 19, 1830	Daniel Bowman—Alsey M. Ellis		Levi Bowman
Oct. 20, 1830	John White—Kesiah Smith		Moses Thompson
Oct. 20, 1830	Carter Jones—Zully Ann Dryman		Jno. Dryman
Oct. 30, 1830	Reuben Jacks—Hannah Irwin		John Irwin
Nov. 4, 1830	David Grayham—Rachel Sands		Wm. H. McCracken
Nov. 4, 1830	Robert Duncan—Sally Campbell		Jacob Taylor
Nov. 11, 1830	Thomas Graynn—Mary Barnes		
Nov. 16, 1830	John L. Howard—Margaret H. Denton		
Nov. 18, 1830	Edward Baker—Lucinda Erwin		
Nov. 24, 1830	Henry Jones—Rebecca Smith		
Dec. 9, 1830	John Smith—Nelly Frake		
Dec. 10, 1830	Davis Henley—Sarah H. Roberts		
Dec. 15, 1830	Abraham McGinnis—Elizabeth Myers		George Reed
Dec. 15, 1830	Walter Chase—Rebecca Elsey		
Dec. 22, 1830	James McCrosky—Rachael Gibson		

Date	Male	Female	Bondman
Dec. 23, 1830	William McAdams—Ealenor McNeal		James Renshaw
Dec. 28, 1830	John Ellis—Elizabeth Shipley		Martin Matlock
Dec. 30, 1830	Samuel Reeser—Ibby Greene		
Dec. 31, 1830	Ira Starnes—Ann McGinty		John Smith
Jan. 1, 1831	Abraham Whitson—Margaret Norris		
Jan. 2, 1831	John Kyker—Rebecca Slyger		
Jan. 5, 1831	John Waddle—Sophia Doak		
Jan. 11, 1831	John J. Wyett—Matilda Toppin		Bartley Boyd
Jan. 20, 1831	Joseph A. Deadrick—Emiline N. Anderson		
Jan. 27, 1831	Thomas Riddle—Jane Rogers		
Feb. 3, 1831	Samuel B. McAdams—Ann S. Duncan		Samuel Keebler
Feb. 10, 1831	Abraham Taylor—Elizabeth McCrey		Shelton Taylor
Feb. 10, 1831	James Deakins—Cloe Martin		
Feb. 19, 1831	Henry Bashor—Elizabeth Bowman		Jno. H. Bowman
Feb. 21, 1831	William Woodruff—Elizabeth Nelson		John H. Nelson
Feb. 26, 1831	John Odle—Nancy Hale		
Mar. 3, 1831	Enoch Brown—Rebecca George		
Mar. 9, 1831	Thomas Brown—Leannora Salt		
Mar. 10, 1831	Edmund Beagles—Manerva Medlock		Levi Bowers
Mar. 11, 1831	Eli Henry—Hannah Haunworth		
Mar. 16, 1831	Ellis H. Duncan—Mary Milburn		Samuel Spurgin
Mar. 17, 1831	Robert Parker—Mary Andes		Ephraim Francis
Mar. 21, 1831	John Hunt—Sarah Nichols		
April 1, 1831	John Mason—Edney Simmons		
April 5, 1831	James Graham—Elizabeth Resser		
April 18, 1831	Caleb Bails—Margaret Iser		Reuben Brown
April 20, 1831	Joseph Mann—Elizabeth Blackburn		
April 21, 1831	David Smith—Sarah Irvin		
April 27, 1831	Alex C. Matthes—Eliza Doak		
May 3, 1831	John Mahoney—Mary Powel		
May 5, 1831	Jeremiah Woodruff—Mary Ann Click		
May 7, 1831	John Moore—Margaret Tucker		
May 15, 1831	Boyer Ford—Sally Chapman		
May 19, 1831	Anson Hodges—Harriett Gray		
May 22, 1831	Christopher Bashor—Elizabeth Hymes		
May 24, 1831	Abraham Brown—Sarah Franklin		
May 25, 1831	John Slyger—Delceney Bacon		Jesse Bacon
May 31, 1831	John Cloyd—Rachall Boyd		
June 2, 1831	Felix Earnest—Rachel Embree		
June 2, 1831	Phillip Mulkey—Ann Duncan		Hiram Hampton
June 7, 1831	Ebenezer Barkley—Mary Taylor		Daniel Barkley

Date	Male	Female	Bondman
June 10, 1831	Landon Carter Hail—Hannah Ellis	John A. Wilds
June 15, 1831	Absolom Goforth—Mary Franklin	
June 21, 1831	James W. Jackson—Margaret Odle	
June 30, 1831	Henry Winkle—Susannah Wilson	George Brown
July 3, 1831	William L. McNees—Eliza Slagle	Charles Slagle
July 7, 1831	James Smith—Elizabeth Brown	
July 14, 1831	James Jones—Elizabeth Keebler	Jacob Keebler
July 19, 1831	William Mitchel—Elizabeth Basket	Reuben Brown
July 21, 1831	Daniel Kenney—Minerva Nelson	
July 21, 1831	David Stevens—Elizabeth Bacon	Samuel Stevens
July 26, 1831	George Russell—Mary Fawbush	Archibald Bails
July 27, 1831	William Hoss—Jane Deaken	John Bayless
Aug. 2, 1831	Henry Stephenson—Luisa Sparks	
Aug. 2, 1831	David Hartsell—Isabella Bayless	
Aug. 3, 1831	John A. Chinouth—Abigail Hunt	
Aug. 7, 1831	Enoch Colsten—Hannah Harrison	
Aug. 8, 1831	William J. Johnson—Mary Hale	John F. Earnest
Aug. 11. 1831	William P. Reaves—Mary Devault	
Aug. 11, 1831	Isaac Bacon—Jane Bacon	
Aug. 13. 1831	Stephen Barnes—Rhoda Brown	E. McLaughlin
Aug. 19, 1831	Mark Foster—Nancy Netherly	
Aug. 22. 1831	Allen Kyker—Malinda Bacon	Mark Bacon
Aug. 23, 1831	Benjamin Shipley—Margaret Miller	Nathan Shipley
Aug. 23. 1831	Ira Bricker—Sally Riddle	
Aug. 24, 1831	Benjamin Birdwell—Margaret Campbell	
			John Ryland
Aug. 27, 1831	Enoch Rector—Polly Malinda Hall	
Sept. 5, 1831	Richard Stuart—Serckey Sanders	
Sept. 6, 1831	Allen Ingle—Eliza Bricker	
Sept. 13, 1831	William Hays—Ann Overholts	Samuel McGehan
Sept. 13, 1831	Thomas Black—Martha Clark	
Sept. 18, 1831	David Leach—Rachel Harvey	
Sept. 20, 1831	Richard Northington—Elizabeth Jenkins	
Sept. 22, 1831	Allen Summers—Sarah Ford	James Quinby
Sept. 27, 1831	Jacob L. Myers—Frances Bell	
Sept. 29, 1831	Peter Cline—Rachel Leonard	
Oct. 1, 1831	Samuel Serber—Eliza Andrew	James Blackeley
Oct. 6, 1831	Jeremiah Chase——Hannah Hail	
Oct. 11, 1831	Alfred B. Dillingham—Delilah Caroline Stephens	
Oct. 10, 1831	Augustine Moss—Ruth Mason	C. E. Kincheloe
Oct. 13, 1831	Joshua Cox—Nancy English	Joshua English
Oct. 13, 1831	John Hays—Hannah Bleakley	
Oct. 20, 1831	Jacob Barron—Jane Murry	

Date	Male	Female	Bondman
Oct. 21, 1831	Saul Overholt—Sarah Smith		
Oct. 27, 1831	John Hunt—Sarah McBride		Isaac Nunn
Oct. 27, 1831	Mishac Hale—Jane Kennedy		Charles Hail
Oct. 27, 1831	Peter Devault—Mary Hoss		
Nov. 1, 1831	John Robison—Jane Brown		
Nov. 3, 1831	Michael Hines—Nancy Nelson		
Nov. 15, 1831	Charles Bacon—Patsey Bean		
Nov. 17, 1831	Berryman Scalf—Rebecca Page		James Wheeler
Nov. 18, 1831	Daniel Coleman—Jane Inser		
Nov. 21, 1831	Andrew L. Herrold—Ann Horton		
Nov. 22, 1831	Joseph Barger—Susannah Williams		
Nov. 25, 1831	Isaac Adams—Sarah Nelson		
Nov. 29, 1831	Ephraim Nelson—Rebecca Skiles		
Dec. 22, 1831	Charles A. Slagle—Eliza Slagle		Wm. McNees
Dec. 28, 1831	Jesse Woods—Margaret McCracken		
Jan. 7, 1832	James Murry—Mary Hopkins		
Jan. 11, 1832	William Whitson—Sarah Eliza McGempsy		
Jan. 17, 1832	Alfred Hays—Harriet Miller		Alexander Hays
Jan. 24, 1832	Solomon McGhee—Lucinda Campbell		
Jan. 26, 1832	Ryley Cannon—Priscilla Bell		
Feb. 9, 1832	John Lyle—Lucinda Borin		J. L. Burts
Feb. 12, 1832	John Konken—Sarah Watts		
Feb. 16, 1832	James B. Cloyd—Catherine Click		
Feb. 21, 1832	Jesse Moore—Elizabeth Tucker		
Mar. 14, 1832	Samuel Baker—Susan Mitchell		
Mar. 22, 1832	James Graham—Catherine Stormer		
Mar. 24, 1832	E. Skelton—Ruby Hale		
Mar. 27, 1832	Abraham Jobb—Sarah Fain		
April 3, 1832	Robert Goff—Mary Ann Starns		
April 19, 1832	William Jobb—Nancy Jones		Laban Jackson
May 1, 1831	Gabriel Sylvester—Maria Fletcher		Joseph Hickey
May 3, 1832	Peter Shipley—Rebecca Sliger		
May 6, 1832	Samuel Harrison—Elizabeth Rineheart		
			Jesse Harrison
May 8, 1832	Preston Shields—Lucinda Nelson		Andrew Givin
May 10, 1832	John Waddle—Delila Phillips		Dan D. Andrew
May 24, 1832	Phillip Bell—Polly Ann Cannon		Adam Broyles
May 24, 1832	Washington B. Barnes—Rebecca Snapp		
May 31, 1832	John Asten—Mary McCracken		
June 7, 1832	David S. Hampton—Margaret Slyger		
June 16, 1832	John Cunningham—Mary Hampton		
June 18, 1832	William Mitchell—Melly Lilburn		
June 19, 1832	Isaac Lamon—Liddy Benley		W. Willett

Date	Male	Female	Bondman
July 5, 1832	Simpson Charton—Sussanah Page		Berry Scalf
July 7, 1832	John Black—Anne Foster		John Coppenger
July 11, 1832	Robert J. West—Leah Crouch		
July 23, 1832	John Perkins—Nancy Cooper		John Andes
July 24, 1832	Jesse C. Wallace—Mahala Bleakley		
Aug. 1, 1832	Nathaniel Sands—Sarah McCall		
Aug. 10, 1832	Moses Moore—Susan Cummings		
Aug. 23, 1832	Levi Pitman—Martha Copp		
Aug. 23, 1832	Spencer H. Watkins—Mary McCoy		
Aug. 30, 1832	William Birdwell—Eliza Jobe		
Aug. 31, 1832	James Whitson—Mary Toney		
Sept. 3, 1832	Uriah Hunt—Mary Kincheloe		Isaac Newman
Sept. 30, 1832	Talbot Jackson—Jane Crow		
Oct. 4, 1832	Gilbert Woolsey—Hannah Tucker		
Oct. 4, 1832	Ephraim Broyles—Mary Broyles		
Oct. 5, 1832	Robert Garvin—Martha Casady		Ephram France
Oct. 8, 1832	Morris Hartsell—Vilett Moore		
Oct. 12, 1832	Charles Cox—Malinda Fitzgerald		W. K. Hulse
Oct. 18, 1832	Alexander Gann—Nancy Campbell		
Oct. 23, 1832	Jeremiah Prather—Mary Ann Snapp		
Oct. 25, 1832	Thomas Gibson—Sarah Martin		
Oct. 25, 1832	David Mitchell—Elizabeth Ingle		
Oct. 25, 1832	Henry McCracken—Rebecca Wood		
Oct. 26, 1832	Peter C. Morrison—Luticia Kelly		Jacob K. Brown
Oct. 30, 1832	Gabriel McIntosh—Amy Nelson		
Nov. 6, 1832	Edmondson Casey—Sarah Hensley		Robert Poor
Nov. 29, 1832	Moses Tworkman—Jane Rector		
Nov. 29, 1832	John Crawford—Elizabeth English		
Nov. 29, 1832	Lewis Cade—Elizabeth Harmon		
Dec. 6, 1832	John Broyles—Lucinda Broyles		
Dec. 6, 1832	Zachanah W. Butler—Susan Range		
Dec. 16, 1832	Bayless Moore—Sarah Stroud		
Dec. 16, 1832	Asbury Lilburn—Sarah Stroud		
Dec. 19, 1832	Samuel Erwin—Mary Parks		
Dec. 19, 1832	Joseph McCracken—Sarah Wood		
Dec. 23, 1832	Joseph Baser—Mary Keener		
Dec. 25, 1832	William Collins—Maria Hunter		
Dec. 27, 1832	George W. Mallone—Nancy Caruthers		
Dec. 27, 1832	James Britt—Nancy Ford		Benjamin Ford
Dec. 29, 1832	William Henry—Leander Jobb		
Dec. 31, 1832	Mulkey Watson—Elizabeth Templin		
Dec. 30, 1832	Barlley Boyd—Lercy Wood		
......,	Thomas Burton—Minerva J. Boyd		Henry A. Wilds

Date	Male	Female	Bondman
Jan. 9, 1833	John H. Hays—Margaret Hays		
Jan. 12, 1833	Abraham Collett—Elizabeth Broyles		
Jan. 17, 1833	Anderson Ryley—Malinda Barger		
Jan. 21, 1833	Joseph Hunt—Polly McAfee		
Jan. 24, 1833	John Gates—Elizabeth Cox		
Jan. 24, 1833	Lemuel Bogard—Hannah Saylor		
Jan. 29, 1833	Phillip Murry—Mary Parker	Peter Kuhn	
Jan. 31, 1833	Charles Bacon—Elizabeth Bacon		
Feb. 3, 1833	Thomas Hammin—Ruth Jiles		
Feb. 6, 1833	Joseph Bellamy—Rebecca Taylor	Lawrence Bowers	
Feb. 9, 1833	Elijah Click—Susan Ralston		
Feb. 12, 1833	Amos Haloway—Mary Hale		
Feb. 13, 1833	Joseph West—Eliza Roberts		
Feb. 28, 1833	John Miller—Hannah Nelson		
Mar. 3, 1833	William Smith—Maria McCray		
Mar. 11, 1833	Charles Whitson—Sarah Davis		
Mar. 11, 1833	William Reece—Malinda Waldrope		
Mar. 14, 1833	Harry Scroggs—Syntha Phillips		
Mar. 14, 1833	Christian Long—Elizabeth Murr		
Mar. 17, 1833	Kenedy Foster—Rebecah Kersewn		
Mar. 20, 1833	Charles Davis—Martha Denton		
Mar. 23, 1833	Thomas Brown—Matilda Murry		
Mar. 27, 1833	Robert Allison—Margaret Williams		
Mar. 27, 1833	Thomas Emmerson—Catherine Jacobs		
Mar. 28, 1833	William Cash—Elizabeth Mears		
April 4, 1833	Joseph Murray—Rachel Brown		
April 9, 1833	Thomas Earnest—Luisa King		
April 15, 1833	Beverage Branum—Mary Ambrose		
April 15, 1833	Pelig Brown—Rosamond Bean		
April 16, 1833	George Allen—Esther Mitchell	Thomas J. Brown	
May 1, 1833	Andrew Walker—Sarah Brown		
May 2, 1833	Abraham Boren—Sarah Robison	Samuel Tipton	
May 2, 1833	John Good—Elizabeth Humphreys		
May 14, 1833	William Spurriers—Martha Ralston		
May 26, 1833	John Ralston—Margaret Starnes		
June 4, 1833	John Richardson—Eliza Broyles		
June 13, 1833	Mathias Coffman—Elizabeth Madlock	John Sherfey	
June 18, 1833	John C. Kennedy—Mary A. Massengale		
July 4, 1833	Peter Skiles—Fanny Arrenduffs		
July 11, 1833	Young Kibler—Margaret Taylor		
July 12, 1833	Richard Bayless—Susannah Giesler		
July 25, 1833	Daniel B. Herald—Elizabeth Andes		
July 27, 1833	Vinett Fine—Marion Carathers		

Date	Male	Female	Bondman
July 28, 1833	George Wattenberger—Nancy Collet		
July 30, 1833	Jesse Hunt—Margaret Hale		
Aug. 1, 1833	Robert Nelson—Lyla Nelson		
Aug. 1, 1833	John Golden—Sarah Pitcock		
Aug. 2, 1833	George W. Gibson—Mary Goin		
Aug. 2, 1833	Peleg Rigsby—Elizabeth Hampton	Gabriel McInturff	
Aug. 11, 1833	Joseph Hale—Sarah Broyles		
Aug. 15, 1833	Absolem Scott—Margaret Huffhines		
Aug. 25, 1833	Jonathan H. Hider—Martha King		
Aug. 26, 1833	Thomas Emmerson—Eliza Greene		
Sept. 1, 1833	David Brannon—Sarah Mitchell		
Sept. 1, 1833	Joseph Rodgers—Rachel Lowrance		
Sept. 2, 1833	William Jack Tedlock—Mary Phillips	Solomon Bailey	
Sept. 3, 1833	Jesse Davison—Phebe Fine		
Sept. 5, 1833	Nathan Shepherd—Ellenner Salts	John Smith	
Sept. 5, 1833	Robert Hert—Sarah Pantor		
Sept. 5, 1833	Hiram Lawrence—Sussanah Krous		
Sept. 9, 1833	Isaac Walker—Sarah Huffhines		
Sept. 15, 1833	William Pugh—Mary Price		
Sept. 19, 1833	Abraham Burket—Dorcus York		
Sept. 30, 1833	Thomas J. Willson—Eliza Embree		
Sept. 30, 1833	John Brown—Rebeccah Deakins		
Oct. 2, 1833	Rich Davis—Rebeccah Andes		
Oct. 2, 1833	John Presnell—Jane Frances		
Oct. 3, 1833	James Bowser—Harriet Keane		
Oct. 5, 1833	Solomon W. Willson—Mary Glaze		
Oct. 9, 1833	Alexander Kerl—Esther Martin		
Oct. 10, 1833	Alfred Stout—Eliza Harvey		
Oct. 11, 1833	William Millar—Susan Eastep		
Oct. 14, 1833	Solomon W. Sellars—Mary Gwynn		
Oct. 20, 1833	Peter Walters—Mary Ann Cressaleus		
Oct. 17, 1833	Robert Bean—Mary Hunter		
Oct. 22, 1833	William Kincheloe—Hannah Jackson		
Oct. 22, 1833	Andrew Gwynn—Abigail Bacon		
Oct. 22, 1833	James Miser—Ann Mitchell		
Oct. 31, 1833	Joseph Oliver—Charlotte Hutson		
Nov. 12, 1833	Alexander Broyles—Elizabeth Mauke		
Nov. 17, 1833	James S. Jobb—Matilda Boyd		
Nov. 18, 1833	John Orindulph—Malinda Miller	Peter Skiles	
Nov. 21, 1833	Herman Hampton—Sarah Duncan		
Nov. 21, 1833	John Davison—Rebecca Fox		
Nov. 21, 1833	John Crouch—Theodocia Hale		
Nov. 22, 1833	Alex W. Wilson—Ann L. Patton		

Date	Male	Female	Bondman
Nov. 23, 1833	John H. Crawford—Susan K. Blair		
Dec. 2, 1833	Isaac Miller—Elizabeth Nelson		
Dec. 10, 1833	George Jackson—Elizabeth Hale		
Dec. 11, 1833	John Duncan—Elizabeth Hampton		
Dec. 21, 1833	James Bleakley—Margaret Hays		
Dec. 24, 1833	Isaac Sawesbeer—Margaret Overholser		
Dec. 25, 1833	Thomas Ferguson—Martha Rogers		
Jan. 1, 1834	James Swaney—Teney Oliver	Adam Casedy
Jan. 1, 1834	Joseph D. Hider—Eliza Ann Nelson		
Jan. 2, 1834	Adam Patterson—Margaret English		
Jan. 9, 1834	James Bacon—Marina Fawbush		
Jan. 9, 1834	Orville P. Nelson—Hannah Hartsell		
Jan. 19, 1834	Ephriam Murry—Elizabeth Snapp		
Jan. 19, 1834	John Grisham—Mary Shipley		
Jan. 24, 1834	Zachanah Brown—Mary Haws		
Jan. 25, 1834	Lewis Martin—Deborah Ryester		
Jan. 28, 1834	Barton Bales—Salita Ann Bacon		
Jan. 29, 1834	Joseph Fraker—Mary Ann Simpson		
Jan. 30, 1834	Hiram Cornett—Sarah Winters		
Jan. 30, 1834	James Gibson—Mary White		
Feb. 6, 1834	Francis Gibson—Jane Martin		
Feb. 6, 1834	John West—Rachel Overholster		
Feb. 6, 1834	David May—Margaret Walter		
Feb. 18, 1834	John Keys—Rebecca Borin		
Feb. 14, 1834	Jonathan M. Brummit—Nancy Martin		
Feb. 22, 1834	Henry Johnston—Mary Ann Hoss	Thomas Crouch
Feb. 25, 1834	Elijah H. Shipley—Margaret Bean		
Mar. 2, 1834	Thomas Crow—Sarah Ford		
Mar. 6, 1834	Wesley Oliver—Elizabeth Duncan		
Mar. 12, 1834	Joel McFall—Deannah Tilley		
Mar. 14, 1834	Simeon Broyles—Mary Longmire		
April 5, 1834	James W. Bowser—Louisa M. Simmons		
April 5, 1834	Young Bayles—Mary Phillips		
April 17, 1834	James Allen—Rachel Bains		
April 22, 1834	Jonathan H. Callam—Nancy Deakins		
May 15, 1834	James Newland—Hester Edgman		
May. 18, 1834	Jacob Watenbarger—Susan Barger		
May 22, 1834	John Devault—Elizabeth Kitzmiller		
May 29, 1834	John D. Cowan—Sarah Jane Buchanan		
June 2, 1834	George Beagles—Margaret White		
June 5, 1834	Watson Swatzell—Barbary Baysinger		
June 10, 1834	David Vance—Mary Jane McCorkle		
June 10, 1834	John W. Doak—Martha C. Payne		

Date	Male	Female	Bondman
July 14, 1834	Israel Browning—Caroline Crouch		
July 24, 1834	David Gibson—Mary Smith		
July 26, 1834	Thomas I. Wyatt—Seranah Cashedy		
Aug. 7, 1834	Robert Nelson—Lucy Nelson		
Aug. 7, 1834	G. W. Willett—Eliza Crookshanks		
Aug. 7, 1834	Alexander N. Cunningham—Margaretta Ann Eason		
Sept. 1, 1834	Nathan A. Peoples—Mary May		
Sept. 4, 1834	Thomas A. Bayles—Sarah Harris		
Sept. 4, 1834	Alfred Davenport—Sarah Swingle		
Sept. 4, 1834	Francis W. Simpson—Mary C. Blair		
Sept. 11, 1834	Thomas Ford—Mahala Fine		
Sept. 14, 1834	Elkena Hoss—Penelope Masengale		
Sept. 16, 1834	Thomas C. McAdams—Cynthia Stephenson		
Sept. 16, 1834	Shepherd Starnes—Mahala Payne		
Sept. 30, 1834	John Baringer—Sabrey Embree		
Oct. 9, 1834	Ephraim Fink—Viney Fawbush		
Oct. 10, 1834	William Reed—Margary Miller		
Oct. 11, 1834	John Mallonee—Phoebe Wheeler		
Oct. 15, 1834	John Cass—Leney Riddle		
Oct. 26, 1834	Hugh Bell—Sarah Higgins		
Oct. 29, 1834	Joseph S. McCall—Malinda Cradock		
Oct. 31, 1834	William Slaughter—Elizabeth Miller		
Nov. 3, 1834	Landon Carter Rogan—Nancy French		
Nov. 5, 1834	Hugh Harris—Elizabeth Jackson		
Nov. 13, 1834	David Mitchell—Martha Fellers		
Nov. 13, 1834	David Williams—Hannah Murry		
Nov. 13, 1834	John Wesleck—Rebecca Shawley		
Nov. 23, 1834	Mordacai Price—Marrian Khun		
Nov. 23, 1834	Isaac Fawbush—Viney Summers		
Nov. 24, 1834	James Collins—Margaret Laudermilk		
Dec. 6, 1834	John L. Rose—Rachel T. Peoples		
Dec. 12, 1834	Ambrose Miller—Christian Morgan		Adam Miller
Dec. 18, 1834	Smith Hunt—Jane Long		
Dec. 18, 1834	William Walker—Mary Brown		
Dec. 18, 1834	Thomas Smith—Lauranna Archer		
Dec. 23, 1834	Lawrence B. Wiles—Jane Wheelock		
Dec. 23, 1834	Thomas Stanberry—Sarah Cass		
Dec. 24, 1834	Cornellia F. Yeager—Salina Hoss		
Dec. 27, 1834	Adam Shipley—Catherine Brown		
Jan. 4, 1835	John White—Sarah Beard		
Jan. 15, 1835	Jacob Ball—Hannah Minerva Boyd		
Jan. 20, 1835	John Keath—Elizabeth Edwards		
Feb. 6, 1835	Charles Sliger—Mary Marks		

Date	Male	Female	Bondman
Feb. 11, 1835	Obediah Chester—Sarah Ellis		
Feb. 15, 1835	Thomas I. Colyar—Mary Bails		
Feb. 22, 1835	Ellis Higgins—Ruth Tilson		
Mar. 5, 1835	Joseph Beals—Mary Sherfy		
Mar. 3, 1835	Alfred Carr—Elizabeth King		
Mar. 10, 1835	John Craddick—Charlotte Mullen		
Mar. 12, 1835	Joshua Green—Sarah Fellows		
April 13, 1835	Freelan Sutton—Lutetia Jordon		Sm'l Bain
April 9, 1835	Joseph Keene—Mary Gibson		
April 15, 1835	Joseph McCracken—Eliza Mitchell		
April 22, 1835	Tipton Ford—Mary Ann Murry		
April 23, 1835	James Conklin—Ruth Ronnels		
April 28, 1835	Joshua Hartsell—Cinthea Bayles		Morris Hartsill
May 26, 1835	Thomas H. Crouch—Julia McEfee		
May 28, 1835	Levi Nelson—Betsy Ann Irwin		
June 2, 1835	Henry Marsh—Scynthia Ann Kirk		
June 3, 1835	Lewis A. Markwood—Sarah Isabella Deakins		
June 13, 1835	William Parks—Nancy Erwin		
June 21, 1835	John Barlow—Mary Freeman		
June 25, 1835	Jacob Naff (or Napp)—Amanda M. Broyles		
June 25, 1835	Isaac Hamilton—Nancy Gott		
July 5, 1835	David Moore—Mary Ball		
July 6, 1835	William Slagle—Sarah Sprigo		
July 30, 1835	Robert Young—Cassy Ann Hendry		
Aug. 6, 1835	Elijah Barlow—Martha Phillips		
Aug. 25, 1835	Robert Kelsey—Rachel Ball		
Aug. 6, 1835	James Flenn—Mary Boyd		
Aug. 9, 1835	Samuel McKeehin—Sarah Watenbarger		
Aug. 11, 1835	George Hoppers—Margaret Bain		
Aug. 11, 1835	Jesse Martin—Nancy Bacon		
Aug. 18, 1835	John Roland—Ann Headrick		
Aug. 20, 1835	Lawrence Bowers—Alsey Mains		
Sept. 10, 1835	Henry McMackin—Esther Stanbury		
Sept. 10, 1835	Bailey Collins—Susannah McGeehan		
Sept. 15, 1835	Francis Robertson—Mary M. Crawford		
Sept. 17, 1835	Jesse Waller—Elizabeth White		
Sept. 17, 1835	George W. Nelson—Martha Yeager		
Sept. 21, 1835	Armstee Wall—Harriet Ross		
Sept. 25, 1835	Levi Bowers—Elizabeth Capps		
Oct. 1, 1835	John Salts—Rachel Barkley		
Oct. 1, 1835	Jesse Nelson—Margaret Young		
Oct. 4, 1835	Pleasant G. Satterfield—Hannah Smith		
Oct. 8, 1835	Elija Wheeler—Nancy Keys		

Date	Male	Female	Bondman
Oct. 14, 1835	Parris Russell—Margarie Cannon		
Oct. 15, 1835	Elias Martin—Ruth Nelson		
Oct. 15, 1835	William L. Erwin—Rebecca Edwards		
Oct. 22, 1835	John McCracken—Dicey Oliver		
Oct. 27, 1835	John Proffit—Nancy Wheelock		
Oct. 22, 1835	Marten Adams—Jane Casaday		
Nov. 5, 1835	John Patton—Elizabeth Collins		
Nov. 12, 1835	William W. Smith—Sarah Bitner		
Nov. 19, 1835	James Harris—Sarah Baskett		
Nov. 26, 1835	George W. Lyons—Ruth Irwin		
Nov. 26, 1835	Abraham Hartsell—Rebecca Lammon		
Dec. 3, 1835	Jordon Lovegrove—Elizabeth Garber		
Dec. 3, 1835	Mark P. Chase—Eliza Campbell		
Dec. 5, 1835	John Million—Alliciadille Bayless		
Dec. 10, 1835	Malan Mahoney—Elizabeth Rogers		
Dec. 11, 1835	John Barkley—Sarah Ann McEfee		
Dec. 17, 1835	Hugh Norris—Hannah Hartsell		
Dec. 22, 1835	William C. Nelson—Julian Slimmons		
Jan. 7, 1836	James McCamish—Martina Bayles		
Jan. 9, 1836	James Hinkle—Susannah Krouse		
Jan. 12, 1836	John McCraskey—Priscilla McCray		
Jan. 13, 1836	David N. Kelsey—Catharine G. McCracken		
Jan. 15, 1835	Malan Summer—Christina Branstutter		
Feb. 4, 1836	Alner Bails—Serena Purces		
Feb. 6, 1836	Alexander Buskill—Amanda Marshl		
Feb. 9, 1836	Stephen Moore—Catharine Holsinger		
Feb. 9, 1836	Daniel B. Proffit—Sarah Range		
Mar. 17, 1836	William L. Cash—Malinda Scalp		
Mar. 24, 1836	William Hale—Elizabeth Biddle		
Mar. 25, 1836	William Purcell—Elizabeth Mulkey		
Mar. 27, 1836	Jesse Duncan—Sarah Dennis		
Mar. 30, 1836	William Bayles—Mary E. M. Lane Beard		
Mar. 31, 1836	Francis Williams—Matilda Stephens		
April 3, 1836	John Gwinn—Barbara Jackson		
April 10, 1836	John H. Gray—Matilda Beard		
April 11, 1836	Britton Phillips—Elizabeth Minerva Bowman		
May 1, 1836	Jacob Boyd—Ruth Mallonee		
May 19, 1836	William Horton—Phebe Tylor		
May 31, 1836	Archibald F. Shields—Mary Hartman		
June 5, 1836	John W. Moore—Nancy Northington		
June 13, 1836	Coderic Cazia—Christina Brown		
June 26, 1836	Silvester Suttles—Margaret Jones	William Nelson
July 1, 1836	Peter Click—Elizabeth Sherman		

Date	Male	Female	Bondman
July 2, 1836	Calvin Woodruff—Elizabeth Million		
July 10, 1836	John Hampton—Rosey McBroom		
July 21, 1836	Nicholas Betner—Mary E. Williams		
July 21, 1836	Ferguson G. Slemmons—Nancy Roberts		
July 26, 1836	John Stephens Collier—Lidia Ballenger		
July 28, 1836	James Nelson—Mary A. A. Atkinson		
Aug. 3, 1836	Daniel H. Kelly—Delila Painter		
Aug. 6, 1836	Washington Million—Susan Mitchell		
Aug. 11, 1836	James Wood—Mary Fulkerson		
Aug. 12, 1836	Calvin Hoss—Amy Deakins		
Aug. 14, 1836	Bernard S. Vaden—Julia F. Sutton		
Aug. 18, 1836	Samuel Sherfey—Fanny Rose		
Aug. 25, 1836	Abraham Casaday—Martha Wilkeson		
Sept. 2, 1836	David Bowman—Emiline Miller		
Sept. 8, 1836	Thomas Waddle—E. Henly		
Sept. 3, 1836	Thomas Galloway—Susannah Sherfey		
Sept. 22, 1836	Benjamin F. Sackett—Evaline E. Aiken		
Sept. 22, 1836	Henry King—Eliza Young		
Oct. 4, 1836	Elijah Colson—Mary Purces		
Oct. 4, 1836	Hugh Shepherd—Mary Sarten		
Oct. 6, 1836	James M. Haygood—Sarah Ann Case		
Oct. 13, 1836	Thomas Collins—Elizabeth Whitson		
Oct. 13, 1836	John Keplinger—Elizabeth E. Hooker		
Oct. 13, 1836	Bluford Ballinger—Sarah Sands		
Oct. 18, 1836	James L. Sparks—Margaret Greer		
Oct. 20, 1836	Isaac H. Bails—Nancy Mulky		
Oct. 20, 1836	Brice W. McFall—Mahala Jane Barnes		
Oct. 21, 1836	Ira Butler—Susan Thomas		
Nov. 3, 1836	John Campbell—Matilda Miller		
Nov. 10, 1836	Jesse B. Hunter—Malinda Catherine Rutledge		
Nov. 25, 1836	Joseph Cline—Margaret Ellis		
Nov. 27, 1836	Allison Hail—Elizabeth Kinchaloe		
Dec. 8, 1836	Allon Bell—Sarah Cannon		
Dec. 10, 1836	William Bricker—Sarah Ingle		
Dec. 13, 1836	James M. Carr—Emiline Hartsell		
Dec. 22, 1836	William Himes—Mary Lemans		
Dec. 19, 1836	John Deakins—Mary Jobb		
Dec. 29, 1836	G. W. Milhorn—Elizabeth Clepper		
Jan. 5, 1837	William Mitchell—Elizabeth Bails		
Jan. 5, 1837	William Sliger—Catherine Lemon		
Jan. 24, 1837	James Armstrong—Nancy Horton		
Jan. 28, 1837	Josiah Parker—Hannah Easley		
Jan. 26, 1837	William Sailor—Rebecca Garber		

Date	Male	Female	Bondman
Jan. 26, 1837	James B. Riley—Elizabeth White		
Feb. 4, 1837	Jeremiah Rose—Sarah Dotson		William Rose
Feb. 9, 1837	James A. Barnes—Deborah Carothers		
Feb. 9, 1837	William A. Cloyd—Elizabeth Cloyd		
Feb. 9, 1837	George Kincheloe—Amanda Brown		
Feb. 9, 1837	Mitchell Roylston—Jane Mashburn		
Feb. 16, 1837	William Barkley—Louisa M. Aiken		
Feb. 22, 1837	Samuel A. Carson—Ealenar S. McCloud		
Feb. 24, 1837	William Smith—Phebe Fann		
Feb. 23, 1837	Francis Bowers—Elizabeth Ann Gyer		
Feb. 23, 1837	Jacob Bowman—Sarah Campbell		
Feb. 28, 1837	William Davison—Sarah Goodman		
Mar. 9, 1837	William Shields—Mary McCrackin		
Mar. 12, 1837	Aman Mitchell—Della Allison		
Mar. 15, 1837	Joseph Boyd—Catherine Spradling		
Mar. 16, 1837	John W. Browning—Matilda Waggoner		
Mar. 14, 1837	James A. Lyon—Adelaide E. Deadrick		
Mar. 23, 1837	James M. Patton—Elizabeth Patton		
Mar. 30, 1837	John Cloyd—Mary Brown		
April 4, 1837	John McCracken—Julia Nelson		
April 5, 1837	James Bell—Eliza Rogers		
April 20, 1837	Stephen Gibson—Elizabeth Ferguson		
April 27, 1837	Zachanah Buckingham—Mary Miller		
May 11, 1837	Dulaney Willard—Caroline Clak		
June 1, 1837	Christian Oler—Nancy Marshill		
June 1, 1837	James Nelson—Margaret Furgeson		
June 8, 1837	Charles Bacon—Nancy Bacon		
June 11, 1837	John Nelson—Nancy Whitson		
June 16, 1837	William M. Lowrey—Julia Eason		
June 17, 1837	John M. White—Rachael Taylor		
June 22, 1837	Jonathan Naff—Elizabeth Massengale		
July 4, 1837	John H. Bowman—Salina J. Broyles		
July 10, 1837	Robert C. Love—Elizabeth Wilkison		
July 26, 1837	Elkano Simmons—Sarenay Ripley		
July 27, 1837	Gabriel H. Odum—Sarah Bean		
Aug. 9, 1837	John Bains—Sarah Bains		
Aug. 15, 1837	John Leach—Phebe Davison		
Aug. 20, 1837	Zachariah Jones—Rhoda Bowser		
Aug. 29, 1837	William Glover—Mary Medlock		
Aug. 30, 1837	David Fine—Viney Dulaney		
Aug. 31, 1837	Isaac Stormer—Catherine Reanner		
Sept. 2, 1837	James Seehorn—Elizabeth Good		
Sept. 5, 1837	James Jobb—Nancy S. Jackson		

Date	Male	Female	Bondman
Sept. 5, 1837	John Slyger—Catherine Sherfey		
Sept. 13, 1837	Samuel Stephens—Eliza Jane Strain		
Sept. 13, 1837	William Cloyd—Julia Norrington		
Sept. 14, 1837	John Miller—Elizabeth Clark		
Sept. 14, 1837	George Davenport—Nancy M. Fain		
Sept. 14, 1837	James Wheeler—Emeline Jobb		
Sept. 19, 1837	E. M. Barkley—Polly Richard		
Sept. 26, 1837	James P. Black—Mary Dyke		
Oct. 1, 1837	Laben Gillis—Nancy Mitchell		
Oct. 3, 1837	Jesse Gray—Manerva Brown		
Oct. 3, 1837	James W. Collam—Elizabeth M. Campbell		
Oct. 5, 1837	John McFall—Elizabeth Laudermilk		
Oct. 12, 1837	Leroy Price—Emily Young		
Oct. 12, 1837	Abraham Gillis—Mary Sailor		
Oct. 17, 1837	George Kennick—Catherine Parker		
Oct. 22, 1837	Robert Garvin—Elizabeth Denton		
Oct. 26, 1837	Joseph Davison—Ibby Jones		
Oct. 30, 1837	Allen Callan—Prudence Brown		
Nov. 3, 1837	John Squibb, Jr.—Sarah Kibler		
Nov. 9, 1837	William Gwinn—Phoebe Whisler		
Nov. 9, 1837	John Ingle—Caroline McCloud		
Nov. 15, 1837	Wilson Edwards—Ann Bradford		
Nov. 16, 1837	Thomas J. Harper—Elizabeth McAlister		
Nov. 23, 1837	Howel A. Hodges—Sarah Ann Crouch		
Nov. 30, 1837	Henry A. Martin—Matilda Brown		
Dec. 3, 1837	James P. Hulse—Ella Krane		
Dec. 4, 1837	Milton Dulaney—Orpha Fine		
Dec. 28, 1837	Peachy K. Snapp—Emeline Nelson		
Dec. 28, 1837	William Bright—Susannah Barkley		
Dec. 28, 1837	Elias Whisler—Anna Jane Gann		
Dec. 28, 1837	Everett Mahoney—Nancy Ann Martin		
Dec. 30, 1837	Emanuel Lamon—Kesiah Hartsell		
Dec. 31, 1837	John Riddle—Lucinda Overholser		
Jan. 7, 1838	George Fink—Mary Keene		
Jan. 8, 1838	Percy Hunter—Elizabeth Crouch		
Jan. 14, 1838	Elijah Harshbarger—Hannah Cox		
Jan. 18, 1838	William W. Ellis—Lucinda Hunt		
Jan. 18, 1838	William P. Hunt—Innetta Harrison		
Jan. 25, 1838	Merriwether Whilock—Sophia Burgner		
Jan. 31, 1838	Charles Mayfield—Jane Adam		
Feb. 1, 1838	Alfred Jenkins—Mary Catherine Krutzer		
Feb. 1, 1838	George W. Vance—Mary Malinda Morgan		
Feb. 1, 1838	Montgomery Kibler—Barbara Garber		

Date	Male	Female	Bondman
Feb. 1, 1838	Frederick Watenbarger—Emeline Charliton		
Feb. 10, 1838	Solomon Stone—Jone K. Hulse		
Feb. 11, 1838	Henry Ambrose—Rhoda Tilson		
Feb. 13, 1838	Jesse Moore—Margaret Good		
Feb. 15, 1838	Stephen Shackleford—Sarah Keene		
Feb. 15, 1838	Martin Crouch—Lucinda Fitzgerald		
Feb. 15, 1838	James L. Jennings—Mary S. Cowan		
Feb. 22, 1838	David Davault—Marie Cox		
Mar. 1, 1838	George Gilley—Nancy Sailor		
Mar. 1, 1838	Abraham L. Gammon—Myra L. Anderson		
Mar. 6, 1838	James Jackson—Carey Chandler		
Mar. 6, 1838	Joseph Bails—Mary Bails		
Mar. 8, 1838	Daniel Ellis—Hannah Bales		
Mar. 15, 1838	John D. Cowan—Mary Barcroft		
Mar. 18, 1838	Jonathan Ford—Jane Stone		
Mar. 22, 1838	Solomon Black—Elizabeth Dykes		
Mar. 29, 1838	William Bovell—Minerva Tylor		
April 8, 1838	Benjamin Bowman—Ann Sliger		
April 12, 1838	James Crabtree—Catherine Page		
April 13, 1838	Adam Broyles—Nancy Mitchell		
April 22, 1838	John D. Murry—Francis A. McAlister		
May 3, 1838	Martin Cash—Catharine R. Carson		
May 5, 1838	Martin L. Hartsell—Margaret Longmire		
May 6, 1838	John Galloway—Betsy Johnston		
May 24, 1838	James W. Duncan—Mary A. Davault		
May 28, 1838	Levi Wilson—Margaret Alexander		
June 1, 1838	Samuel Rogers—Alsay Wine		
June 3, 1838	Jacob Hilbert—Esther Garber		
June 14, 1838	James Haws—Mary Kibler		
June 29, 1838	Ezekiel Hammitt—Phoebe Chandler		
July 1, 1838	Joseph Hannah—Sarah Ann Chanler		
July 26, 1838	William Walters—Nancy Cummings		
July 27, 1838	Uriah Slaton—Evelina Kurts		
Aug. 2, 1838	Joseph Overholser—Charley West		
Aug. 2, 1838	Robert Mitchell—Catherine Bails		
Aug. 5, 1838	Charlton Williams—Darcus McGhee		
Aug. 9, 1838	Henry Slagle—Elizabeth Williams		
Aug. 9, 1838	J. Taylor—L. Humphreys		
Aug. 18, 1838	Newton Hamit—Emily Hedrick		
Aug. 23, 1838	Samuel Fitzpatrick—Elizabeth Hodge		
Aug. 24, 1838	William Hartman—Lucensia Register		
Sept. 3, 1838	Seth Kincheloe—Barthena McPherson		
Sept. 7, 1838	Daniel Horton—Mary Jane McCall		

Date	Male	Female	Bondman
Sept. 10, 1838	Alfred Hays—Mary J. Landon		
Sept. 9, 1838	Zacanah Chandler—Malinda Milburn		
Sept. 12, 1838	D. H. Tucker—Mary Marten		
Sept. 12, 1838	Joshua Vaughn—Edy Myers		
Sept. 12, 1838	James Elsey—Sarah Hulse		
Sept. 13, 1838	Joseph McCully—Mariam Royston		
Sept. 19, 1838	Abraham Barnes—Sarah A. Carothers		
Sept. 20, 1838	James D. Hunter—Sarah Martin		
Sept. 28, 1838	D. M. Miller—Rachael Wheelock		
Sept. 25, 1838	Cyrus Broyles—Hannah McCray		
Sept. 30, 1838	John Good—Martina Hutchison		
Oct. 1, 1838	William Hatcher—Mary Boothe		
Oct. 4, 1838	Samuel Douglass—Ann Starr		
Oct. 5, 1838	Archibald A. Mathes—Christianna G. Cowan		
Oct. 5, 1838	Abner White—B. J. Waggoner		
Oct. 10, 1838	Flower Mullins—Chrisey M. Mullins		
Oct. 11, 1838	Isaac Tapp—M. Hampton		
Oct. 18, 1838	John Purcell—Susan Furgeson		
Oct. 18, 1838	David Good—Mary Ann Broyles		
Oct. 21, 1838	James Casaday—Rebecca Brummett		
Oct. 23, 1838	Thomas Biddle—Nancy Ann Hamilton		
Oct. 29, 1838	David Sellars—Nancy Garber		
Oct. 29, 1838	Matthew Bleakley—Charity Craddick		
Oct. 30, 1838	James White—Margaret Yeager		
Nov. 1, 1838	Robert L. Blair—Martha R. Cunningham		
Nov. 8, 1838	Henry Fawbush—Maria O'Donnell		
Nov. 8, 1838	Joseph Boothe—Elizabeth Collett		
Nov. 18, 1838	John Douglass—Nancy Jobe		
Nov. 18, 1838	Carder Stone—Elizabeth Stone		
Nov. 22, 1838	Rufus Cobb—Nancy Hail		
Nov. 22, 1838	Andrew J. Doherty—Mary W. Phillips		
Nov. 29, 1838	John Dugger—Malvina Morris		
Dec. 4, 1838	Joseph Simpson—Adalade Bayles		
Dec. 4, 1838	Castillian Fitzimmon—Rebecca McGreer		
Dec. 8, 1838	Montgomery Range—Malinda Broyles		
Dec. 12, 1838	Charles Headrick—Margaret Salts		
Dec. 13, 1838	Isaac ......linger—Mary Yeager		
Dec. 16, 1838	Hugh A. Crawford—Caroline Cox		
Dec. 20, 1838	Andrew M. Workman—Nancy Rector		
Dec. 26, 1838	Elkanah Chandler—Nancy Hammett		
Dec. 30, 1838	William Mullinox—Sarah Leab		
Jan. 3, 1839	James Keebler—Susannah Garber		
Jan. 10, 1839	Joseph Good—Ruth Irwin		

Date	Male	Female	Bondman
Jan. 17, 1839	J. Sherfey—E. Hail		
Jan. 20, 1839	W. Grimsley—A. Proffit		
Jan. 30, 1839	Jacob Tipton—S. White		
Feb. 3, 1839	C. Cox—Sarah Ann Billingsley		
Feb. 10, 1839	L. Colyer—M. Spears		
Feb. 11, 1839	William G. Gardner—M. G. Chester		
Feb. 13, 1839	W. Brown—Betsy Byerly		
Feb. 17, 1839	C. Oliver—E. Starns		
Feb. 17, 1839	J. H. Cox—H. E. Copas		
Mar. ...., 1839	William H. Hodges—L. Hale		
Mar. 10, 1839	J. Clark—L. Ellis		
Mar. 12, 1839	J. Andes—C. Walters		
Mar. 15, 1839	Jacob Brown—Susan Mitchell		
Mar. 17, 1839	L. Gray—M. Banner		
Mar. 19, 1839	A. G. Mason—L. Ryland		
Mar. 22, 1839	A. Brommit—Catharine Cosiah		
Mar. 26, 1839	Job Clark—T. S. Nelson		
April 3, 1839	J. W. Allen—C. K. Maxwell		
April 18, 1839	C. Gibson—M. Mallone		
May 12, 1839	J. Kimmery—E. Missinger		
May 6, 1839	William White—Nancy White		
May 7, 1839	J. Price—E. Young		
May 9, 1839	William W. Humel—S. Hartman		
May 16, 1839	James Hale—Elizabeth Barkley		
May 19, 1839	Robert L. Stanford—Mary Taylor		
May 17, 1839	M. Monteeth—L. Page		
May 20, 1839	I. L. Fowler—E. Mitchell		
May 25, 1839	F. Hail—M. Bacon		
June 16, 1839	William Ellis—E. Soul		
June 18, 1839	W. G. Gammon—J. A. Aiken		
June 27, 1839	D. Howel—N. McIntire		
June 27, 1839	J. Kagle—M. Oden		
June 27, 1839	Adam Myers—Amanda Waesner		
July 14, 1839	Joshua Vaughn—S. Stevens		
July 20, 1839	Isaac Smith—Rebecca White		
July 27, 1839	T. A. R. Nelson—A. E. Stuart		
Aug. 6, 1839	J. H. Pain—M. Wheelor		
Aug. 8, 1839	William Gwinn—S. A. Hail		
Aug. 11, 1839	King Lewis Roberts—Melvina Thacker		
Aug. 13, 1839	I. Whitlock—N. Wheelor		
Aug. 17, 1839	I. G. Leach—C. Ander		
Aug. 21, 1839	William Tinker—E. Klouse		
Aug. 26, 1839	I. T. Basket—A. Hartman		

Date	Male	Female	Bondman
Aug. 26, 1839	Nathan Kiker—E. Broyles		John Booth
Aug. 28, 1839	I. Crouch—E. Mains		
Aug. 27, 1839	William Greenway—M. McMacken		
Aug. 31, 1839	William Jackson—Nancy Crow		Jonathan Ford
Aug. 26, 1839	J. W. Earnest—N. Patton		
Aug. 30, 1839	Davis Lawson—I. A. Christie		
Aug. 22, 1839	Isaac L. Reeves—Martha Miller		
Sept. 15, 1839	I. Barns—E. Cloyd		
Sept. 16, 1839	Z. N. McCall—E. Hodge		
Sept. 19, 1839	J (or L.) Fain—S. Jackson		
Sept. 23, 1839	M. C. Snapp—M. E. Falls		
Sept. 29, 1839	William Mowdy—N. Warren		
Sept. 29, 1839	James Murr—A. Ragen		
Sept. 29, 1839	Andrew Swicegood—Sabray Owen		
Sept. 29, 1839	Jacob Hider—Elizabeth Bean		
Oct. 1, 1839	Richard Humphreys—M. Hartman		
Oct. 10, 1839	J. Humphreys—D. Smith		
Oct. 12, 1839	J. Collins—M. Morgan		
Oct. 13, 1839	M. Milburn—Polly Harris		
Oct. 15, 1839	M. H. Garland—R. I. Odwin		
Oct. 17, 1839	S. Houston—E. Barnes		
Oct. 20, 1839	James Brown—Margaret Harvey		
Oct. 24, 1839	Peter Northington—R. Cloyd		
Oct. 27, 1839	C. Allen—C. Kiker		
Oct. 31, 1839	William McCracken—Jane Patton		
Nov. 4, 1839	William Frakes—Susannah Hartman		
Nov. 7, 1839	J. Duncan—A. Goins		
Nov. 15, 1839	William L. Humphreys—J. Gwinn		
Nov. 18, 1839	J. Bricker—E. Sisk		
Nov. 16, 1839	I. Harris—N. Hensley		
Nov. 21, 1839	I. Elsey—N. Cox		
Nov. 10, 1839	David B. Pickens—Rebecka A. Keen		
Nov. 24, 1839	A. Howard—E. Price		
Dec. 14, 1839	N. Goins—C. Price		
Dec. 25, 1839	H. Denton—I. C. Stevens		
Dec. 26, 1839	J. Kimmery—E. Morgan		
Dec. 31, 1839	S. M. Hunt—E. Ellis		
Dec. 29, 1839	J. R. Pain—R. Barnes		
Jan. 9, 1840	D. Galloway—K. Dykes		
Jan. 16, 1840	A. Peoples—E. Melvin		
Jan. 23, 1840	Samuel Davault—S. Galloway		
Jan. 25, 1840	W. McKinsey—E. Martin		
Jan. 30, 1840	J. Pearson—C. Collins		

Date	Male	Female	Bondman
Jan. 30, 1840	Allen Range—A. Crouch		
Feb. 3, 1840	William Brown—Rachel Clouse		
Feb. 3, 1840	T. F. Arrington—L. G. Bell		
Feb. 4, 1840	William Sherman—A. Spradling		
Feb. 6, 1840	George Gray—R. A. Chinouth		
Feb. 13, 1840	N. H. Chenouth—E. Hodges		
Feb. 13, 1840	L. F. Stephens—S. Curry		
Feb. 13, 1840	L. Moore—M. A. Briggs		
Feb. 18, 1840	N. S. Snapp—M. A. Payne		
Feb. 18, 1840	L. C. Hail—Louisa Hail		
Feb. 23, 1840	Calvin Cox—Phoebe Barns		
Feb. 26, 1840	H. Baulton—D. Haws		
Feb. 26, 1840	Asa Bayles—Delila Good		
Mar. 5, 1840	W. Mathes—S. Mathes		
Mar. 8, 1840	A. Sherfey—M. Gharst		
Mar. 8, 1840	William Wycuff—E. Rollins		
Mar. 10, 1840	John S. Gains—M. Pursell		
Mar. 12, 1840	G. Goin—S. Kincheloe		
Mar. 12, 1840	E. S. Mathes—E. A. McKee		
Mar. 17, 1840	W. Morrison—E. Thornburgh		
Mar. 24, 1840	R. B. Ellis—E. L. Dodge		
Mar. 30, 1840	Shan Chase—Margaret Brown		
April 2, 1840	William Haws—M. Hall		
April 4, 1840	Solomon Rollins—M. Vaughn		
April 6, 1840	S. B. Hammer—E. Range		
April 15, 1840	W. Embree—E. Blair		
April 16, 1840	Nathaniel Curtis—B. Rhinehart		
April 19, 1840	S. Miller—A. Headrick		
April 23, 1840	Moses Jobb—R. Hampton		
April 25, 1840	Jesse Bacon—P. Barnes		
April 30, 1840	J. P. Gaby—M. Harshbarger		
April 30, 1840	J. Hartman—E. Bowman		
May 5, 1840	B. Jones—M. Dickeson		
May 16, 1840	A. Pearson—M. Brown		
May 21, 1840	S. C. McAdams—E. Harvey		
May 28, 1840	C. Presly—E. Gibs		
May 28, 1840	M. Martin—R. Kiker		
June 1, 1840	Samuel Sharfey—N. Gharst		
June 4, 1840	J. Hodge—M. L. Curtis		
June 6, 1840	Thomas G. Brown—S. Patterson		
June 10, 1840	J. J. Hite—M. Mowdy		
June 12, 1840	M. Smith—E. Smith		
June 14, 1840	J. Rose—R. Brown		

Date	Male	Female	Bondman
June 14, 1840	William Spring—M. Sprinkle		
June 27, 1840	William Collins—L. Furr		
July 12, 1840	M. Hudson—S. Click		
July 13, 1840	L. C. Rogers—F. Literal		
July 14, 1840	C. Bishop—M. A. E. Nelson		
July 23, 1840	James Loyd—M. Hays		
July 28, 1840	John Cowin—Larrina Thomas		
July 30, 1840	L. McNabb—M. D. Whaley		
July 30, 1840	Elias Brown—Susan Clark		
Aug. 6, 1840	P. Walker—P. Cunningham		
Aug. 16, 1840	J. Suttles—A. Howell		
Aug. 12, 1840	Thomas Lamon—L. Heines		
Aug. 13, 1840	Jesse Cottell—M. A. Hoss		
Aug. 18, 1840	George Bacon—Mary Irwin		
Aug. 19, 1840	John Cossass—N. Birdwell		
Aug. 20, 1840	James Murry—S. Birdwell		
Aug. 18, 1840	Samuel Hicks—P. A. Rogers		
Sept. 1, 1840	Charles Duncan—E. Hoss		
Sept. 1, 1840	William Lane—Nancy Rose		
Sept. 3, 1840	J. Hicks—M. Carson		
Sept. 3, 1840	Charles Range—E. Klipper		
Sept. 9, 1840	Z. Runnels—Sarah Miller		
Sept. 10, 1840	John Little—N. Davis		
Sept. 15, 1840	John Roberts—T. Carter		
Sept. 15, 1840	John Grimitz—L. Keesee		
Sept. 17, 1840	J. C. Perkins—Sarah Cooper		
Sept. 17, 1840	A. J. Hoss—S. Duncan		
Sept. 18, 1840	Jesse Pate—M. A. Crowley		
Sept. 23, 1840	D. Good—P. C. Gann		
Sept. 25, 1840	M. Short—Sarah Ruth		
Oct. 1, 1840	R. F. Ferguson—S. J. Russell		
Oct. 3, 1840	Isaac Basher—Mary Clark		
Oct. 7, 1840	Benjamin Cary—Nancy Headrick		
Oct. 13, 1840	John Haws—R. Hail		
Oct. 14, 1840	James Cade—Susannah Hale		
Oct. 14, 1840	James Leach—N. Denny		
Oct. 15, 1840	Robert McCracken—Jane Jones		
Oct. 15, 1840	L. T. Irwin—E. Broyles		
Oct. 15, 1840	J. R. L. Johnston—E. Bierly		
Oct. 20, 1840	William Hail—S. Buckingham		
Oct. 20,1840	William Oliver—P. Starns		
Oct. 22, 1840	William Ronnels—P. Hillens		
Oct. 22, 1840	F. H. McCally—M. Gibson		

Date	Male	Female	Bondman
Oct. 22, 1840	W. L. McNeese—E. Carson		
Oct. 22, 1840	A. A. Doak—Sarah P. Cowan		
Oct. 27, 1840	I. Miller—Sarah Simmerman		
Oct. 28, 1840	William Irwin—C. Stout		
Nov. 1, 1840	Thomas Moore—I. A. Hampton		
Nov. 1, 1840	W. Reeser—C. Miller		
Nov. 5, 1840	S. W. Miller—E. A. Range		
Nov. 10, 1840	Samuel Bowman—M. Hail		
Nov. 12, 1840	Richard Cass—Sarah Klepper		
Nov. 15, 1840	S. Sisk—L. Cook		
Nov. 21, 1840	John B. Brown—N. Philips		
Nov. 26, 1840	Hiram Sellars—M. J. Morris		
Dec. 10, 1840	Wade Hampton—M. Hunt		
Dec. 24, 1840	I. R. Melvin—N. E. White		
Dec. 24, 1840	Eli Hicks—S. Carson		
Dec. 27, 1840	John Hulse—B. Murray		
Dec. 29, 1840	James Patton—Sarah A. Barkley		
Dec. 30, 1840	W. Hughes—N. Colyer		
Dec. 31, 1840	J. S. Doff—C. Campbell		
Dec. 31, 1840	M. Paxton—N. Pursell		
Dec. 31, 1840	J. Sherfy—Sarah Hoss		

www.ingramcontent.com/pod-product-compliance
Lightning Source LLC
Chambersburg PA
CBHW070257290326
41930CB00041B/2629